The Essential Guide on How to be A Hoe

Slaytor Jackston

SLAYTOR'S
PLAYHOUSE

THE ESSENTIAL GUIDE ON HOW TO BE A HOE

Copyright © 2021 by Slaytor Jackston.

All rights reserved. Printed in the United States of America. No part of this book may be used or reproduced in any manner whatsoever without written permission except in the case of brief quotations embodied in critical articles or reviews.

For information contact : Slaytor's Playhouse, LLC
info@slaytorsplayhouse.com
http://www.slaytorsplayhouse.com

Cover design by Vikncharlie on Fiverr
Edited by J.S. Living
Introduction written by J.S. Living
Book description by Missfrancis on Fiverr

ISBN: 978-1736631904 (full text; paperback)
       978-1736631911 (half text; ebook)
       978-1736631928 (Prose from a Soul Seeking Justice; ebook)

First Edition: February 2021

10 9 8 7 6 5 4 3 2 1

Acknowledgements

I owe a great deal of thanks to those who came before. To my ancestors who endured so I will have the voice to speak, to my parents who provided me with love throughout the years, and to my friends and family who have provided me with endless support: I say thank you for all you have done. Special thanks to my friend Jaleesa for both editing this book and writing the introduction. You are a phenomenal writer and friend. For those who have purchase this book, I invite you all to purchase hers as well. Find her work under her author name J.S. Living.

Table of Content

Preface .... p.   i
Introduction .... p.   v
Chapter 1: If It's Not for You Don't .... p.   1
Chapter 2: Consent... p. 13
Chapter 3: Hoeing is Not Always Prostitution .... p. 29
Chapter 4: Safety is a Priority.................................. p. 49
Chapter 5: This is Not *the Game* .... p. 53
Chapter 6: Judgement and Sexual Positivity.............. p. 63
Chapter 7: Where to Start....................................... p. 71
Chapter 8: Building a Roster................................... p. 79
Chapter 9: Benediction of Hoeing .... p. 85
About the Author... p. 89

Preface

If you have purchased this book, I am grateful for your support. This book is, by no means, a way to slut shame or degrade any individual. If this is the reason you purchased this book, I am sorry to inform you that this book is not the one for you. If you are expecting to read about "how to play the 'dating game'", this is not the book for you. If you are reading this to find out how to be a pimp, a playa, a hookup artist, or the number one "fuck boy/girl", this is not for you. Now, if you are looking to embrace your sexuality and live your best sexually positive life, this may be the book for you.

I cannot guarantee that all the information you read will not be offensive, but I can guarantee that you will learn something new during your adventure through the text. If you do come across something that you find offensive, reflect on why you find it offensive. Is it something that you are not comfortable with? Whatever the reason, the intent is to educate and not to offend.

In reading this book, you will come across the term "consent" often. Using the definition from Merriam-Webster, consent, in its verb form, is to give assent or approval. As a noun, consent is compliance in or approval of what is done or proposed by another. If at any time while reading this book, or in your personal life, you forget what consent means, I have provided you with a definition. If that definition is too elaborate for you, here is the most basic definition I can provide: NO MEANS NO AND YES MEANS YES.

If you have yet to figure it out yet, I am big on consent and support consent in every form it may take. If you are a nonconsensual pussy grabbers, you might as well turn away now. This book is most definitely NOT for you. A person's body is their temple and however they wish to dress it, maintain it, or construct it, is completely up to them. If you have a problem with that, then you need to educate yourself and learn to love yourself. More than likely, it is the lack of self-love and your own ignorance that forces you not to let others live their lives. Now that I have made this statement, let us discuss the premise of the book.

As you see from the book's cover, I use the word "hoe" rather than the term "ho". We are all aware of the difference between the two. One is a gardening tool and the other is referring to much more. A "ho" is slang for the term "whore". And it is this term *whore* that gives me the most issue. When was the last time you looked into the etymology of the term? Here is a brief summary of what you will find. The term has been around, in some capacity since the 13th century, possibly before then. This usage is primarily female centered, though it later includes male prostitutes in the 1630s. Because of the heavy association with the female person through history, religion, and media, when one uses the word "whore", the most common image associated with the term will likely be that of a woman.

By definition, a whore is a male or female who engages in sexual acts for money. It is also defined as an unscrupulous person. This definition continues my worries and furthers my desire to not use the term "ho". There will be more of this to come, just you wait. The term unscrupulous is an adjective that means unprincipled. Because someone is "a whore", they are to be seen as someone who lacks principles. With that being said, every individual who is referred to as a "ho", root word being "whore", is considered someone without principle. This opens the floodgates for actions that perpetuate slut-shaming and validates the ideologies behind it. In a sense, it validates victim-blaming. In a world where we enjoy seeing someone get their "just desserts", it only make sense that an unscrupulous person must pay for their actions. And this, is a mindset that I do not follow nor support.

At this moment, I am going to step high and proud to my soap box and speak my final words on why I choose to use the term "hoe" instead of "ho". That reason has much to do with the etymology and spelling of the word "ho". The noun "ho" gained its meaning in 1993 and is considered American English slang. It is the African American vernacular pronunciation of the word whore. Trust and believe, I enjoy and appreciate African American Vernacular English. It appears it was done in such a way to dumb down the complexity of black vernacular. I get it. Black people do not commonly pronounce the "r" sound when it comes at the end of a term. But there is no difference in sound when one says "hoe" or "ho". Did it sound differently when you read it in your head? I think not. In addition to this, conjugating this word as a verb seems quite incorrect without utilizing the same rules as the word "hoe". For example, one will not be "hoing", they will be "hoeing".

I know it seems like a petty reason to dislike a word, but there are several terms within the English language that has multiple meanings to them, which includes slang, that are spelled the same. For example, the word "peace" is one such term. When it comes to a salutation, it is not spelled "peece" or "peese". It is as though the slang became dialect rather than a duality of a common language. One may also argue that this may have been a way to isolate African American vernacular as a lesser form of language. You tell me.

For the purposes of this book, you will find the spelling of the word "ho" as "hoe". Hoe is not to be confused with a singular sex, gender, or sexual orientation. In my opinion, anyone is capable of being a hoe. With that being said, there is absolutely nothing wrong with one choosing to live a hoe-based lifestyle. If that is not your fancy, that is okay. IT IS NOT MEANT FOR YOU. Let me advise you now, what you are not going to do is judge those who choose to live this life. No matter what your walk of life may be, there is someone who does not like the way you live it. Remember this: that is their problem, not yours; however, this does not give you any right to judge the lifestyles of others. If you do not agree with it, that is fine. Continue to live **your** life. You have your own life to live, do not be selfish and attempt to live another's life.

Introduction

When I was younger, I was sexually harassed by my cousins; and I never stopped to think how that harassment affected my other life choices. As an adult, when I look back on those moments, I realize that it had larger implications than I could ever imagine. Had I realized those connotations earlier, I might have made different choices in terms of my sexual experiences. On that note, what I want to discuss with you all is this gem known as *The Essential Guide on How to be a Hoe*. Ya'll, I wish that I'd had a book like this when I was younger! It delves into all sorts of topics—most notable to me is that of consent, toxic masculinity, and mental health—and gives the reader information on how to do better.

This book is broken into nine chapters and each one hit a little differently (in a good way). Chapter One, titled "If It's Not For You…Don't", discusses the personal issues that readers like you and I may have when it comes to sex positivity. The caution that it provides is literally in the title: if the book isn't for you, then don't read it. In all honesty, I think everyone should just accept that this is a book made to make you uncomfortable, challenge your beliefs, and promote a sexual positive lifestyle. That said, I hope that it is for you.

For me, Chapter Two: Consent is where it's at. There are so many issues today regarding consent. Whether you're a man, woman, non-binary, etc. this chapter is relevant to you. It discusses toxic behaviors—like sexual coercion and personal obligation in regard to sex—as well as how consent goes both ways. Perhaps it's because people have taken away my agency in the past, but I believe that a discussion on consent and what it means is ALWAYS warranted. If you're looking for a chapter that educates and raises awareness of the importance of consent, then this is definitely the chapter for you.

Chapter Three, "Hoeing is Not Always Prostitution", and Chapter Four, "Safety is a Priority" are sort of like a combo deal. You can't talk about one without the other (okay, you could, but you'd be missing half the conversation). This chapter hit home for me because, as a woman, I was always taught that my body is my temple. And, while true, it was always meant as a way to deter me from my curiosity of sexual encounters. I didn't grow up in an uber religious home, but I did hear enough lectures about how I would be doomed if I lost my virginity before marriage or how experimenting with the same sex would send me straight to hell (even as an enlightened adult who knows better, I wonder if these things are true; that's how often it was drilled into me). For those who had this experience growing up, don't fret. Chapter Three explains the meaning of hoeing (and why it's okay to do it) and Chapter Four explains how to have safe sex. In other words, they give you permission to hoe around, but safely.

Chapter Five: This is Not *the Game* is also pretty dope. It talks about and elaborates on *the game*" (if you've ever watched *How I Met Your Mother*, you know what I'm talking about). In the simplest of terms, this chapter describes how to have mature interactions with other adults. Whether you're monogamous or polyamorous, it's imperative that you discuss the terms of your relationship with each of your partners. Doing this doesn't necessarily mean that you're stepping out (this book ain't about that life) and playing *The Game*, but it does touch on how to be responsible when it comes to those who are in your care.

If you're looking for something that will help you discover your "best life", Chapter Six: Judgement and Sexual Positivity might be right for you. Undergrad me would have killed to read this chapter—she desperately needed it. After all, I wasn't the type to hang out, party, and sleep around. But it wasn't because I didn't want to. It was because I had been taught that those were actions of men and women who didn't know what they wanted out of life and couldn't be bothered to settle down. Obviously, those are antiquated thoughts, but it's hard to get out of your comfort zone when you've been stuck in your own head for so long. If I'd had something to read that told me it was okay to be sexually positive, to want to try things like group sex or joint masturbation, well…let's just say that it wouldn't have taken me as long to realize my own self-worth.

And, speaking of living your best life, Chapter Seven: Where to Start breaks down the ground rules of being/becoming a hoe. It's the lasagna of the book because it bakes all the other layers (in other words, chapters) together to help you develop your own conscientious rules. Rules that will help you become a better person. It'll also provide some guidance on how to build your roster. Coincidentally (okay, not really), Chapter Eight is titled "Building a Roster" and exists to encourage you to manage your lifestyle and—if you so choose—multiple partners. Now, me, I have a hard enough time managing one partner, so managing multiple partners sounds like a lot. If you're able to do it, bravo! I applaud you because it does NOT seem easy. In any event, if you purchased this book so that you could be a true hoe, then these two chapters are the only ones you need. Of course, you did purchase the entire book, so you might as well read the other chapters (especially Chapter Two, I cannot stress that one enough).

Last, is Chapter Nine: Benediction of Hoeing. This chapter is a summary of all the other ones and stresses the necessity of progress and growth. Which, duh, this is a self-help book, so those two things are a given.

So, now that you have an overview of what this book is about, I want to tell you how grateful I am that I was able to write this introduction for you. Whether you're heterosexual, part of the LGBTQIA+ community, monogamous, polyamorous, saving yourself for marriage, or hoeing, I hope that you can gain something from this book. Though uncomfortable at times, I promise you this: When you finish this book, you'll be able to drop some knowledge on everybody. Thank you for your support!

~J.S. Living

Chapter 1

If It's Not for You…Don't

I have dedicated years trying to come up with a solid definition for the term "hoe". I have asked friends, family members, and even passersby how they define the term. Today, I still do not have a solid definition for the term. Similar to the definition of leadership, there are as many definitions for the word hoe as there are people willing to define it.

We have developed the mentality that we want a classy person in the streets but a freak in the bed. From what I have learned throughout my sexual experiences, it does not take much to obtain the status of a freak. Sometimes, that involves having more than one sexual partner and testing out your sexual techniques. Yes, it is true that you can test out new things on one person but is that person willing to experiment with new things. For example, let us use Tyler Perry's film *Temptation: Confessions of a Marriage Counselor*.

For those who have not seen it, watch it. It is a great movie and has been out since 2013. Since it has been out for some time now, I do not care about spoiling the film. In this film, Judith—played by the extravagant Jurnee Smollett—is married to her childhood sweetheart Brice (Lance Gross). There comes a point in their marriage where things become stagnant. Judith changes her style and all, but Brice does not notice. She even asks to have sex in different positions, and she is denied. She is not being satisfied at home and has an affair. Due to the affair, Judith and Brice's marriage falls apart and Judith, unfortunately, contracts HIV. The film makes it obvious that Brice is happily married and has a family while Judith is all alone and...let me stop right here. There are some issues that I need to unpack.

Though I enjoyed this movie, I hate that Judith is punished with HIV for doing the same thing many men do on a regular basis in cinema and in reality. Furthermore, the movie portrays Brice as the victim solely because his wife cheated.

Let me say this now before anyone gets in their feelings by that last statement, I am a firm believer that if you are not being satisfied in your relationship discuss this with your partner first. If they are not willing to adjust to your needs, then you have every right to leave an unsatisfying relationship. I do not condone cheating. However, in this case, she went to her husband and addressed her concerns. She wanted a change with her husband prior to seeking a change with an outside party. All Judith wanted was a good dick down from her husband that was not missionary, and he said no. Female and submissive sexuality is not embraced the way it should. It is time to reclaim that definition of hoe and make it something positive and empowering. Again, if it's not for you, then don't.

As mentioned in the preface, I am not a fan of the spelling "ho". Much of this is due to the history of the term. Some of that history I dislike is the definition itself. An unfortunate amount of people I have asked to define the word provided a definition that singled out women only. This is something I do not agree with. The characteristics that many often describe can be attributed to either a male or female. Some of the definitions I received include: "a woman who has a lot of sex", "a promiscuous woman" (*how original*), "a woman with low morals", "a woman who has sex with more than five sex partners throughout her life because the thing in her pants is sacred and must only be given to her husband", and, a personal favorite, "bitches with a loose pussy". And the definitions go on from there. I am going to take this moment to say these two things: 1) if it is not for you, do not make it for you. Who are you to judge? 2) Hoe-ness has no gender!

I am going to come back and address some of these definitions in a second, I just want to highlight another perspective in this argument: sexual position within the gay community. If this is out of your comfort zone, find another book or skip to another paragraph because this is a topic that needs to be discussed. I have asked some gay men what they define as a hoe and many of the definitions had a similar trend. Like most individuals who attributed hoe-like behavior to women, the hoe-like behavior is attributed to the bottoms rather than the tops. Also, let the records show that members of all sexual positions were asked, from strictly oral to verse to tops. I must say the verse guys were a lot more adamant about it.

For those who are unfamiliar with these terms, a bottom is a guy who typically receives anal penetration, a top gives it, and the verse guy does either or; it is shorthand for versatile. I cannot say that I was extremely shocked by this in any way. It appears that people tend to think that those that take on the *supposedly* submissive sexual role are not allowed to embrace sex as much as those that take on the "dominant" role. This brings up that old inconsiderate question, "Which one's the man in the relationship?" Let me just tell you this now, a bottom can be dominant. A woman can be dominant.

Any individual can be a hoe, and there is absolutely nothing wrong with that. If it is not for you, then keep on moving.

A hoe is not a woman nor bottom that has a lot of sex. *What does that mean to have a lot of sex?* I, for one, enjoy sex. I have had bad sex. I have had a lot of mediocre sex. And I have definitely had some amazing sex. I am sure I can say the same for you as well. If you have not, that is fine. I am not going to judge you; however, if you are judging me, *who asked you?* When people define a hoe as someone who has a lot of sex, I think they have not been having enjoyable sex. Sex should be pleasurable and mutually enjoyable. This includes vaginal sex, anal sex, oral sex, frottage, or whatever fetishes you have. I am including BDSM in this as well, because that is a different kind of pleasure that I am not going to go into right now; however, BDSM is a full spectrum of sexual experiences.

"A lot of sex" is an entirely vague statement because it does not give you a sense of whether there is a quantity in mind or a frequency. It is, simply, a lot. If I had sex with my partner eight times in the span of five hours, is that enough to make me a hoe? If I had sex with my partner 730 times within a year, am I a hoe? Just for those who hate math, that averages out to twice a day for a year; adjust accordingly for a leap year. I cannot say for sure that makes me a hoe. I could say, however, either we both have a lot of time on our hands or we are excellent at time management.

For those who say that a hoe is someone, specifically a woman, with low morals, jump off your high ass pedestal. I hope you land in your own business because that is what you need to mind. There is no set guide to morals and values. Yes, we can all agree with the concept that killing someone is wrong. But many of those who agree with this same statement support wars, death penalty, or may make a statement that "all child molesters deserve to die". But again, killing someone is wrong. One cannot push an argument about what is morally right and not be a hypocrite in some other fashion that goes against that same moral. Would you like examples?

We know that pedophilia is not okay, some would say morally wrong (something I agree with). Yet, there are family members that you would not trust near your children. Why is it that Uncle Bob or Aunt Betty are not in jail? Next, we say abortion is morally wrong. However, we are willing to make the argument that it should be provided for victims of rape or incest. Guess what, it is still an abortion. You're just adding unneeded qualifications and exploiting the trauma that someone may have experienced. It is not your obligation to add qualifications on how someone wants to treat their body. Are you making laws that restrict access to food to obese individuals? It is their bodies. It is their choice. You know that feeling you have right now. That feeling is known as cognitive dissonance. You were presented with a conflict that contradicted your own beliefs and assumptions.

Our next definition is quite detailed. A hoe is a woman who has sex with more than five sex partners throughout her life because the thing in her pants is sacred and must only be given to her husband. I feel as though the person who gave me this definition is one shy of number five. But, let us unpack this definition. Why five? I stopped counting after I reached ten. Don't judge me, I decided to wild out when I lost my virginity. I was 19 and in college. On top of this, I have been researching sexuality since age 10. This does not mean porn. I am talking about human anatomy, Kama Sutra, and safe sex practices.

That said, when defining a hoe, is it necessary to include the number of sexual partners? I understand there is a health risk with having multiple sexual partners, which is why I promote safe sex. Take a look at Judith. She had sex with 2 men in her life and ended up with HIV after having sex with guy number 2—opposed to others who did not get a sexually transmitted infection (STI) until partner number 52. Not saying that it is a guarantee that someone will contract an STI from hoeing, it is a possibility. You can contract a disease or infection with a low number of partners. Clearly, the number of partners does not matter.

I am sure those of you who may want to take the abstinent or biblical standpoint would argue that you should save it for marriage. Here's a fact. Abstinence-only sex education does not discourage teens from having sex. Comprehensive sexual education would benefit the youth more than abstinence-only education. Also, abstinence until marriage is not for everybody. Some want a test drive before they make the investment that marriage often brings.

As for the comment that the thing within a woman's pants is sacred, I agree. What we all have in our pants is sacred—regardless of the type, size, or shape of the sex organ. But we often use the term "sacred" in a way to shame others. For example, there are sacred temples all over this earth and people are invited to gaze upon its wonders. We say nothing. But when that sacredness is used to describe sexuality, most definitely in terms of the feminine body, it becomes the highest of sins to gaze upon it. This is not to say that one should not be selective in whom they allow to gaze upon their temple, but one should not feel ashamed of it either.

When I choose to have sex with someone, I call it a blessing. I blessed that individual—be they male or female—with my sexual talents and my body. I know what I bring to the table and what I bring is amazing. Call me cocky if you must. But I ask for feedback and I like to hone my sexual craft. Keep in mind, however, I do not hand out blessings to any and everybody or whenever they want. Take God for example. There are billions of people on this planet and God is able to bless them whenever God sees fit. Therefore, if I choose to bless 5, 10, or even 50 different people in my lifetime with my body, that is not for you to judge. As Mary Mary once put it, "It's the God in me". Now, if that is something that is not for you, you do not have to practice what I preach.

Now, let us discuss my favorite definition. A hoe is a bitch with loose ass or pussy. I adjusted this definition to be more inclusive of the LGBTQ+ community. I have heard this definition multiple times in defining hoes.

Let me just go out and say that the vaginal canal and the anus are strong muscles and they both bounce back. If you are having sex with someone and they feel "loose", rather than attempting to make them feel bad because they are not "tight" enough for you, ask yourself if you are full enough for them. Are you truly pleasing them or are they unsatisfied and appeasing your ego with fake moans? If you feel like they were loose, why not ask them to be completely honest with you and provide feedback on your stroke game. You never know how helpful this advice can be. Also, having sex does not make a person's vagina or anus "loose".

On the flipside, anal tearing and vaginal tearing can be a contributing factor. Muscle tearing can affect the elasticity of the vagina or anus. This can be due to dryness of the vaginal canal or the lack of using sexual lubricant. For those out there who are upset if it is not "wet", carry lubricant just in case. Be prepared. Relying on your vagina owning, sexual partner to provide the lubrication with their natural secretions is not always beneficial.

As for the anus, I recommend always using lubricant. The rectal canal does make its own form of lubricant, mucus, but it is not enough to prevent tearing. This can also be a contributing factor to painful anal sex. There should be a minimal discomfort from anal sex, not excruciating pain. If you are feeling more pain than pleasure, I recommend that you find a partner that is willing to take their time to allow your muscles to relax.

No matter which form of sex one decides on, vaginal or anal, ensure that your partner's muscles are relaxed. These pornos are lying to you. Stop hurting your partner by just jabbing your penis inside. If they are running from you at the start of sex, then you probably violated their insides. I understand the desire to beat a back out, but you can still do so by easing into sex. Even if it is a one-night stand or random hookup, you do not have the authority to literally tear up another person's insides.

Keep in mind, for those who may be a tad bit sore from minor tearing, your temple will snatch back after a few days without sex. There are literally people out here taking a whole fist, or bigger, inside of them and all walls are stable. There are vaginal creams and gels that help with rejuvenating the vaginal canal. Feel free to invest in those if you wish. As for the anus, I am still looking for something that can help in a similar capacity as the gels and creams. However, allowing the tears to heal naturally or using hemorrhoid creams may help in the meantime. Also, do not take this as medical advice. Reach out to your primary care official for recommendations and treatments.

Now that we know what does not define a hoe, what is a decent definition? It is a gardening tool. **Duh.** I am only joking. A hoe is a noun, an adjective and a verb. A hoe (noun) is any individual, regardless of gender identity, who chooses to live a sex positive lifestyle free of the judgement and shame of outside influencers and embraces and owns the full extent of their sexuality. It (adjective) describes an individual who chooses to live a sex positive lifestyle free of the judgement and shame of outside influencers and embraces and owns the full extent of their sexuality. For some to hoe (verb), they must be participating in activities that are sex positive and are existing in a manner free of the judgement and shame of outside influencers. To hoe (verb) means to embrace and own the full extent of one's sexuality. *Now, are you ready to take the journey and learn how to be a hoe?*

I want to take a moment to remind you that if hoeing is not for you, then you do not have to hoe. Also, you do not have to be a hoe to be sex positive. The two are not synonymous. There is no set definition of what sex positive is, however, it does refrain from shaming others and their sexual practices. One does not even have to like sex to be sex-positive. If you do not like sex, that is fine. There is absolutely no judgement. Whereas, hoeing, for the purpose of this book, more so Chapter 7, is for those who enjoy sex and wish to embrace it. I ask those of you who wish to be a hoe to take a moment to self-reflect.

Ask yourself, why do you want to be a hoe? What are you looking to get out of this journey? Are you trying to fill a missing void? Find love? Do you just enjoy sex? Are you trying to get over someone? The answers to these questions can make a huge impact on your journey. For example, I do not recommend someone live their best hoe life when they are dealing with hurt from a former relationship. This can do more harm than good in the long run. I recommend having a true love for oneself before attempting to live this lifestyle. This will be explained in further detail in Chapter 7. Until then, make sure you are being honest with yourself when you are self-reflecting on these questions.

You should now ask yourself about how long you are planning to participate in the hoe lifestyle. Are you planning on doing this for a year? 6 months? For the rest of your life? It is not necessary to have a set timeframe. Truth be told, you can even be a hoe within a monogamous relationship. It does not matter. The length of time only matters if and only if it matters to you?

Another question for you to answer is whether it is for a special occasion? For example, some people may want to hoe because they are going out of town and just want to see what the town has to offer in the sexual department. Sometimes the occasion may be that you are finally going to see that person you have had feelings for and have not seen in years. Maybe it is because you are moving and not returning, and you wish to take the time to see those that you never got around to seeing. I have done that one before. Seize the day. Why spend time wondering what it would be like when you can see right now?

The last question you should ask yourself is what are you comfortable with doing? What are your do's and don'ts? This will also be discussed later in Chapter 7. As of right now, think about your comfort zone. Is there anything that you are not into? What are the things that you are into? How well do you know your body? Do you love yourself? Is there anything that you wish to change? These are important questions to answer when learning about your sexuality. We all experience sex different and all want different things performed during the act.

A word from experience, do not expect the qualities and beliefs that you possess to be the same for others. For example, you may enjoy giving oral and may find someone who hates receiving it but is willing to provide that for you if you desire. You may find people who match you perfectly and others that you may have to adjust with/for. There may be someone out there that you find extremely attractive, but you do not mesh well together sexually—and that is ok.

There will be a lot of trial and error. However, there will also be multiple opportunities for success. There are many poisonous fish out there ruining the quality of fish in your ocean or sea. When you catch a few bad ones, do not throw them back in the water to accidentally end up on your hook in the future. Put them off to the side. The quality fish that fits your standards are waiting to be caught.

Slaytor Jackston

Chapter 2

Consent

(**WARNING**: Some aspects of this chapter may cause discomfort or may become triggering to the reader)

Consent is a difficult concept to understand. I only say this because many make it hard. If you ask me, it is simple. The only way for a person to consent is for them to give an enthusiastic yes. Anything outside of this, is not consent. "Yes" is the only thing that means yes! However, this is a book about educating, therefore, let us educate ourselves on the topic of consent.

Remember when I mentioned that little thing about cognitive dissonance? If you do not remember, please make your way back to Chapter 1. When discussing consent, we are often faced with our own cognitive dissonance. You may have the desire to mention that I am incorrect and your pre-existing beliefs are the only truth that exists. I am going to tell you this now, your beliefs may be fictitious. If they are, that is okay. Now, you will have new information that will assist in unlearning harmful information. We all have things we are ignorant about. If this so happens to be one of those things you are ignorant about, I am happy that I am able to assist in educating you.

Just for a sense of credibility for those who may question this information, I am versed in the subject of consent. I have been studying rape culture and consent since 2014. Within this time frame, I have earned a bachelor's degree and a master's degree, and I am currently pursuing my doctorate. My research toward obtaining my master's degree focused on rape culture within the collegiate environment. As for my dissertation, the focus is the same but more focused on campus leaders/influencers, such as fraternity and sorority organizations. I will include a list of reading recommendations at the end of this section for those interested in learning more about rape culture and consent.

First and foremost, what is consent? As mentioned before, consent is an enthusiastic yes. It is the yes you give someone when they ask you would you like $100. It is the yes you give to someone when they ask you if you want to go on a friends' trip or go watch a movie. That yes you provide to the previous requests is the same yes you should be looking for when it comes to sexual encounters. Absence of the enthusiastic yes does not equal to a maybe or a definite yes. Absence of a yes is a no. There are no hidden secrets. The only way for a person to say yes is for them to articulate yes.

Some would argue that if one wishes to be as clear as possible with what they are consenting to, the individual should use a consent contract. Though I do not use those myself, just know this is an option for those who may desire its use. It would be remiss of me not to mention this now, but if someone choses to use a consent contract, their consent can be retracted at any time. Think of the consent contract as a subscription to a premium service. The only difference is when one unsubscribes, or consent is withdrawn, the premium you paid would be refunded and the benefits end immediately. There is no loss for either party and no boundaries were violated. By this point, I hope you know where this chapter is going. If you do not, you will definitely know soon.

Consent is giving one's approval. Consent occurs when one person voluntarily, or enthusiastically, agrees to the proposal or desires of another. Think about a marriage proposal. When one partner proposes to their potential fiancé, the potential fiancé must provide their consent to become engaged to marry. Remember this example for later discussions within this chapter. Also, keep in mind what I mentioned about cognitive dissonance. Now, back to this marriage proposal scenario. To be respectful of gender identity, and to assist those who may not grasp the full spectrum of gender identity, I will be referring to the partner who proposes as Sam and the potential fiancé as Jordan.

As I have mentioned before, Sam has made the decision to propose to Jordan. Jordan enthusiastically says yes and agrees to become engaged to Sam. This is consensual. Now, let us shift the environment of the proposal. Imagine your version of Sam and Jordan and place them in a public setting, such as a mall. Now, prior to digging into this scenario, remember consent can be withdrawn and "no" is also an appropriate answer for a proposal.

As we are imagining Sam and Jordan at the mall, be sure that the mall is crowded. Sam begins to make their move to propose to Jordan. The crowd stops what they are doing. They pull out their phones and begin to record this declaration of love. The energy of the crowd is exciting and anticipatory for a response. Sam has the biggest and happiest of smiles on their face. Jordan begins to blush. Jordan looks around and sees the many people that are watching the life changing moment unfold. Jordan seems speechless for a few moments and then says no. Sorry if you're upset with this response in this scenario. It was literally foreshadowed within the last paragraph.

Sometimes, when a person says "no" it is not a rejection of the person, but the proposal. When this happens, there may be a need to have a discussion with your partner to see what is going on. Sometimes, your partner may not be ready to have the conversation about why they said "no", and this is okay. They probably just need time to get to the point to have the conversation. Their "no" is more about them than it is about you. This is a time for you to listen and learn. Marriage is a big decision for many people. It is life changing. There is a possibility your partner is not ready for marriage or being engaged. Maybe they are dealing with more deep-rooted concerns that they may need help processing before they make the decision to marry. Whatever the case may be, they need the time to articulate their feelings.

Let's rewind the scenario. This time imagine Jordan says yes to Sam's proposal. Sam wraps Jordan in a warm embrace. The surrounding crowd begins to clap and provide their congratulations to the couple as they pursue their new milestone. Later that day, shortly after returning from the mall, Sam continues to tell Jordan how happy they are to now be engaged. Sam states how they cannot wait to inform parents. Jordan, who happens to be close to the door of the couple's shared apartment, catches the attention of Sam. Jordan states they are sorry and do not wish to hurt Sam. Jordan says they are not ready to be engaged and the pressure of the crowd made Jordan say yes to the proposal. Jordan did not want to reject Sam in front of the crowd out of fear of embarrassing Sam.

If anyone is upset by this outcome, again, I apologize. This is a plausible scenario. Though this is a yet another example of a person retracting their consent, there is more to the situation than that. Peer pressure and coercion can influence a person to say yes; however, it is not consent. If you must convince or persuade someone to say yes, then it is not true consent. Let this be stated now: there is no difference between persuasion or coercion. The only difference, based on definition, is coercion's use of force. However, coercion is not always forceful—more of that to come later in the chapter, outside the upcoming paragraph.

Let us return to the scenario between Jordan and Sam. Sam is noticeably hurt by the rejection of their proposal. Sam then goes on the following rant:

> "Jordan! How can you do this to me? I thought you loved me. You said you didn't want to embarrass me. Well, I'm clearly embarrassed. Who do you think you are to say no to me!? As though I don't pay for your food, your clothes, your shoes! No, you're going to marry me and that's the last I'm going to hear of that! Think about it. You have nowhere else to go. You can't afford to be on your own. I own everything that is you! And we are getting married. End of discussion."

This is an example of toxic, aggressive behavior. If your image of Sam suddenly shifted into a male figure, I am happy to inform you that you have the ability to identify toxic masculinity. Back to the scenario. For most, this scenario is uncomfortable. This is coercion at its finest. With coercion comes control and a sense of power. Sam did not physically force Jordan to stay and marry them, Sam made a forcefully restricting reality where Jordan has no way out of the marriage. Be mindful, Jordan did not reject Sam, just their proposal. Jordan is not ready for the level of commitment that comes with an engagement or marriage. This is not consent. Forced consent is not consent. Persuaded or coerced consent is not consent. It is not consent if there is no enthusiastic yes. Consent is a thing, and it is important. Consent cannot be stolen or taken. Consent is not something that can be implied. Consent is something that one party gives to another. Also, if they are not a legal adult, they cannot consent to any sexual act no matter how mature the **CHILD** may seem. By this point, I hope you know what's next. If you do not know then it is rape. Rape is the next topic.

Rape is defined as being forced sexual intercourse inclusive of both psychological coercion and physical coercion. In addition to rape, other aspects of this subject must be explored—including sexual assault and sexual violence. Sexual assault is the full range of physically forced, verbally coerced, or substance-incapacitated acts such as kissing, touching, or vaginal, oral, and anal penetration. Since I have referred to it several times now, let's define sexual coercion. Sexual coercion is any unwanted sexual activity that happens when a person is pressured, tricked, threatened, or forced in a nonphysical way. Lastly, sexual violence. Sexual violence is any sexual activity when consent is not obtained or not given freely.

This section is uncomfortable for a reason. Rape is uncomfortable. Rape is traumatizing. Rape is life altering. Rape is something that should never be validated, which contributes to the rape culture many have. Much of the information in terms of statistics presented below can be found on the Rape, Abuse, and Incest National Network (RAINN) website.

According to the current statistics, as of October of 2020, every 73 seconds, an American is sexually assaulted. To put that into perspective, if commercial breaks on a typical channel lasts 3 minutes each break, this means there is a minimum of 2 people raped or sexually assaulted on every commercial break. If that makes you want to skip commercials and go to your preferred streaming service in order to get your mind off the subject, please be mindful that if one were to watch a 45 minute commercial-free show, then roughly 36 people have been sexually assaulted or raped within that time frame. Uneasy, but I am going to take this chance to mention that current statistics estimated an average of 433,648 victims aged 12 or older experience rape and sexual assault each year in the United States. Apparently, young people are not as safe as some would believe them to be.

Younger people, those under the age of 30, are at the highest risk for sexual violence. People who are within the age range of 18 and 34 make up 54 percent of sexual assault victims. But sexual violence can happen to anyone at any age. Though this age group makes up the majority, this does not mean sexual violence is absent within the minority. I mention this in order to tackle a topic I often see online when the topic of sexual violence appears, which is also a tie-in to the next sexual violence statistic pertaining to a person's legal sex. I use the term legal sex because most statistics may mention male or female, but there is no true way of knowing if the recorded data is based on the victim's reported gender or the gender presented on a person's legal documents or identification when reported within the general population. If someone has more information on this, please educate me on this topic. I would appreciate it.

1 out of 6 women are estimated to have been a victim of an attempted or completed rape within her lifetime, whereas men are estimated at 1 out of 33. I must first acknowledge that 1 rape within any category is too many. Among college students ages 18 to 24, college women are 3 times more likely to be a victim of sexual violence compared to the general population. College men, on the other hand, are 5 times more likely to be a victim of sexual violence compared to the general population of men. Additionally, 21 percent of college students that identify as transgender, genderqueer, or nonconforming have been sexually

assaulted. Seems to me as though colleges are not as safe as most think.

In reviewing the statistics, women have a higher chance of being raped than men, however, men are still being raped. When there is a post on social media of a person highlighting the plight of women being sexually assaulted, it does nothing for the fight to end sexual assault by stating the fact that "men are raped too". As a man who has been sexually assaulted in the past, I can tell you now, just about all advocates against sexual violence know. Advocates know men are victims of sexual violence and are victimized by those of the same gender and different gender expressions. Contrary to what some may believe, the fight against sexual violence is not a fight against men. It is a fight against rapist and victimizers, which means ALL rapist and victimizers regardless of gender expression. However, due to the high volume of sexual violence against women—a term I am using to be inclusive to those who identify as trans women—and feminine presenting genderqueer and nonconforming individuals, this is why the argument seems to be female heavy. I am here to tell you all voices are being heard in this fight.

For anyone who wishes to educate themselves more about sexual violence and review updated statistics, I recommend visiting RAINN's website. There is so much more to the topic outside of what has been mentioned thus far. Sexual violence has a lasting impact on the victims. It is within our families, our churches, our prison system, our armed forces, and sometimes our relationships. Sexual violence is widespread, and perpetrators must be held accountable for their actions. Now that sexual violence has received an introduction, I feel as though it is time to discuss sexual violence and consent. This section may be triggering for some and I recommend that you do what is best for your mental health. The purpose for much of this chapter and this book is to educate. For anyone who may need the resources, I will make sure I include RAINN's contact information and webpage within the recommendations list.

Remember our friends Jordan and Sam? I feel as though it is time to bring them back. Remember, their image is solely within your hands. Just a reminder for those who might have been affected by the information load that was the previous set of paragraphs. Consent has to be given. It is not implied. It is not yours to take. For those who do not know, consent is sexy.

Imagine Jordan and Sam once more. They are sitting on the couch. The couple are watching a show they both enjoy. The vibes within the room seems warm, comforting, and joyous. Both Jordan and Sam are enjoying each other's company. If the atmosphere can be described as a feeling, the atmosphere is just *right*. Jordan places their arm around Sam's shoulders and pulls Sam closer. Sam chuckles. Jordan begins to kiss Sam. Sam kisses Jordan back. Jordan then begins to kiss down Sam's body. Jordan's kisses come close to Sam's naval area. Jordan lifts Sam's shirt. Jordan then begins to unbutton Sam's jeans. Sam whispers to Jordan, "Wait". Jordan continues to kiss around Sam's pelvic region. Sam lets out a moan. By this point, Sam's underwear is at their ankles. Jordan performs oral sex on Sam until Sam orgasms.

What is missing from the former scene? If you do not know what is missing within this situation, that is okay. If you are experiencing that feeling as though you are back in class and everyone else seems to know the answer, but you do not, that is okay. You are not the only person that did not know that consent was the one thing missing within the sexual encounter. The scene is an example of sexual violence.

If you are feeling as though I may be wrong, that is on you. Feel free to have the conversation with whomever you wish in order for someone to validate your perspective on the scene. However, at the end of the day, my statement remains true. *Is this an appropriate time to bring back our friend cognitive dissonance?* In the previous scene, Jordan did not receive Sam's consent. I understand some may argue that the mood seemed *right*. Let me be the first to tell you, what's *right* for you is not *right* for another person. The feeling of *right*-ness is not something that can be implied. The feeling of *right*-ness is not something that replaces consent. The feeling of *right*-ness is the opportunity to engage in conversation to see if the atmosphere is *right* for both parties.

Consent seems to be a hard topic to understand, but it really is not. Consent is only a hard topic to discuss because we live within a rape culture. It is hard to see what is missing around you when your culture tells you that it is never needed and is not present. To all of you who wish to live the life of a hoe, understanding consent is your first step. I would love to end this chapter here, but, unfortunately, there is still more that needs to be understood about consent in terms of sexual violence.

Rewind the previous scene. Jordan's arm is around Sam. The two have consented to making out. There is mutual passion throughout the room. Sam is now lying on their back. Jordan smoothly runs their hand down the front of Sam's body as though Jordan's fingertips are cotton ball hairs. Jordan begins to kiss near the naval area. Jordan then begins to unbutton Sam's jeans. Sam whispers to Jordan, "Wait". Jordan stops. Jordan looks upward and locks eyes with Sam. "Are you ok? You don't want oral?", asks Jordan. Sam responds, "I'm not really feeling it tonight. I'd rather just make out some more and cuddle." Jordan replies, "I'd like to do that too. I'm here to please you. I also want to please you this way too. I'll make it quick." Sam pauses for a second. Sam responds, "I guess".

I know some of you reading this scene and thought, "who the fuck says no to oral?" Those who thought that may be having a chuckle right now and that is ok. It is a somewhat funny statement. Outside of that, oral sex is pleasurable, but it is not pleasurable for all people. We all possess different sexual interests and that is ok. Sexuality, and the way sexuality is expressed, is quite complicated. But that is a deep conversation for a different book.

This is yet another example of sexual coercion. This is not consent. Jordan does not respect Sam's wishes and attempts to persuade Sam into having oral sex. This is not appropriate behavior, and this is not consensual. Also, *I guess* is not an enthusiastic *yes*. I often wonder if the sexual coercion would be reduced within relationships if we all became more comfortable with rejection.

Sexual violence is a draining topic to discuss. It is tiresome. I am tired of writing about it. However, it is a topic worth discussing and we should tire ourselves so much that we do not allow it to continue. This is a topic that I am passionate about and I am tired of it. Because I am so tired of it, let me go down a full list of items that are considered sexual violence.

- If your partner is intoxicated in any way and you have sex with them, it is considered sexual violence. People often ask if both parties are intoxicated is that still considered sexual assault? It is still considered sexual assault according to the law. That is not up to me to define for any person. Additionally, if your partner informs you that they wish to have sex with you later in the evening after a night of partying and drinking, do not have sex with them. First and foremost, they would be intoxicated at the time of the sexual act and that is rape under the law. Whatever sexualized being that comes home to you, do not have sexual intercourse with them.

Make sure they are ok and let them rest. Secondly, remember, consent can be retracted. Just because someone consents to sex at 4:00 PM does not mean they would be consenting to it at 8:00 PM (i.e. when friends cancel plans on each other). Things change. Because your partner is intoxicated, they are unable to provide consent.

- If your partner consents to sex where one or both parties must wear some form of protection, it is considered sexual violence if any party removes their form of protection without the informed consent of their sexual partner. For example, if you are having sex with your partner, and you remove a condom without your partner's knowledge, this act is a type of sexual violence. As a rule, do not engage in any sexual activity if you have desires to trick someone into having your preferred sexual encounter. At the end of the day, at least one party, the victim, did not have the opportunity to provide consent to the unprotected sex.
- With the previous example, I have the need to broaden my example. Because of the use of the word condom, I feel as though some minds became gender specific. I just want to remind readers that perpetrators of sexual violence are not specific to any gender, race, religion, sexual orientation, or age. Essentially, if sexual violence is likened to a corporation, it is an equal opportunity employer. With that being said, if your partner is under the impression that you are using a form of birth control and you are not, that is a form of sexual violence. Before anyone throws the book, forms of birth control include condoms (both male and female), the pill, a vasectomy, the IUD, the shot, so on and so on. I only mention this to say birth control is a two-way street,

similar to the responsibilities which come along with birthing a child and thereafter.

- If either party has any life-altering disease, please inform your sexual partner. If you do not, it is considered a form of sexual violence. I encourage all to get tested on a regular basis and communicate with your sexual partner(s) if there is some disease in which you and your partner must discuss. Though some are curable, this does not mean the disease is not life-altering. I do not possess the authority to declare whether or not a disease is life-altering. What may seem meaningless to one person, may be significant to another. If you need an example, think about the COVID-19 pandemic.

There is just so much about consent. I may be able to podcast about consent for hours. But that is also a conversation for another day. I feel as though we are all at an understanding of consent. Some might be angry, others may feel validated, and maybe some were even able to heal. Who knows what you have experienced while reading this chapter? But this chapter must come to a close. I would not consider my job complete if I do not tackle some common myths about rape. Whatever you take away from this section is what you take away. Enjoy!

- Rape can happen within a relationship, which includes marriage.
- Your partner does not belong to you. They are a WHOLE person too.
- A person's clothing or dancing does not mean they are asking for sex.
- Expressing one's sexual desires is not exclusive to cisgender heterosexual presenting men. Stop the slut-shaming!

- Sexual assault does not always include physical bruising (just in case you did not come to that conclusion yet).
- Men are capable of controlling their sexual behaviors.
- Falsely reported sexual assaults do occur, but, the probability for false claims are low. (Believe women. Believe children. Believe the survivors)
- Sexual violence happens often! (in case you did not catch that memo yet)
- If the person is under the age of consent and sexual acts occur, it is sexual violence. If you are an adult coercing/influencing a minor into keeping secrets, being in a relationship with the stipulation that sex would not happen until they are of legal age, or engaging in anything sexual, it is sexual violence. Leave kids alone!
- Those who have some form of a disability are twice as likely as those without a disability to be sexually assaulted.
- Prostitutes and sex workers can be raped (foreshadowing).
- There are resources available to those who have been a survivor of sexual violence.

Literature Recommendations

Sexual Coercion. (2019). Office of Women's Health. Retrieved from https://www.womenshealth.gov/relationships-and-safety/other-types/sexual-coercion

Violence Prevention. (2020). Sexual violence. Center for Disease Control and Prevention. Retrieved from https://www.cdc.gov/violenceprevention/sexualviolence/index.html

Rape Culture. (2020). Retrieved from https://www.csbsju.edu/chp/health-promotion/sexual-violence/rape-culture

Hayes, R. M., Abbott, R. L., & Cook, S. (2016). It's her fault. Violence Against Women, 22(13), 1540–1555. https://doi.org/10.1177/1077801216630147

Resources
Rape, Abuse, and Incest National Network
- https://www.rainn.org/
- 800-656-HOPE (4673)

National Suicide Prevention Lifeline
- https://suicidepreventionlifeline.org/
- 800-273-8255
- Text GO to 741741 (Crisis text line)

American Psychological Association
- https://www.apa.org/helpcenter
- https://www.apa.org/helpcenter/crisis

Chapter 3

Hoeing is Not Always Prostitution

I want to start this chapter off by highlighting one thing. This chapter is not a means for shaming prostitution. As mentioned before, being a hoe is all about sexual positivity and uplifting others. I do not shame any individual who takes part in sex work, especially those who consent to it on a regular basis and have their consent respected. Additionally, for those sex workers who are being forced into having sex, my heart goes out to you and I will do my best to fight for your liberation and peace of mind. I am fortunate enough to say I am able to empathize with you all, but empathy is not the same as experiencing what you all have gone through. I am not going to force myself to imagine the entirety of what you all have experienced, or at which point those negative experiences began, but I do hope that those who have been forced into sex work are able to find freedom and happiness. With that being said, I feel as though it is time to dive into the chapter.

When a person is called a *hoe*, it is understood that the individual is either promiscuous, classless, or a tool for the use of pleasuring others. It is, for the most part, negative. It amazes me how people can understand how insulting the term can be, yet are silent about the struggles forced upon our sex workers and prostitutes. I separate these terms because each word has its own societal view. For example, a sex worker is often used when referring to actors within the porn industry, strippers, and escorts. However, when we use the term prostitute, we often think of someone who sells their body on the street corner. But what is the difference between the two? If you ask me, the main difference is consent and ownership.

I want to shatter the myth of what a prostitute looks like. In media, a prostitute looks like the example above. In reality, a prostitute is a child, a teenager, an adult, a spouse, a partner, a friend, an emotionally damaged person, a person overcoming adversity, someone vulnerable, a prostitute looks like all of us. There is no set image of what a prostitute looks like or who they are. However, I would say a prostitute is a survivor that is constantly being victimized. A prostitute is a person who is not free to do what they wish. For some, they are comfortable with all I have said because "at least they're getting paid" or "if they don't like it, they can quit". To those who think this, you are a part of the problem and I want you to go to therapy in order to process through your own hurt and trauma. Additionally, go back to Chapter 2 and reread the lesson on consent.

For those who have money as their religion, I will not judge you, but do not force your religious practices onto others. For those who are not within that religion, money does not mean you own a person's livelihood. Even when they are employed, looking at things on a broader spectrum, an employee still has a right to live their life while on the clock and off the clock. You are hiring an employee, not a slave. You are hiring a human being with actual feelings and a life outside of work, not a piece of furniture or device that works when you tell it to work. Your employee is not a microwave. They are not an Alexa, Siri, or Cortana. They are a human being who just so happened to be employed by you. Treat them accordingly.

It confuses me how often people dismiss the plight of victims of human trafficking, which is inclusive of prostitutes and hired laborers. Just because a person is being paid for a service, this does not mean they are not entitled to respect. Additionally, just because a person pays for sex, does not mean they are consenting to being raped or required to have sex with the person. Additionally, for the laborers, just because a person is making minimum wage under the law, does not mean they are being paid fair wages in terms of the work they do or able to live a comfortable life.

I think it wise to mention that I am an advocate for sex workers and prostitutes. I wish to see them protected under law. Additionally, I wish to see more resources allocated to those who are being sex trafficked. I am not an expert in all things human trafficking; however, I will be utilizing resources that range from personal experience, which includes my personal shortcomings in reaching out for help on the behalf of others and stories that have been shared privately and publicly. I will also be utilizing the Department of Health and Human Services website. For some, the information I share will make you uncomfortable. For others, the information may be triggering. For those who are triggered, I will always recommend contacting a mental health professional, so you are able to process through those feelings. For those who are uncomfortable, I ask that you lean into your discomfort in order to learn and provide aid to those who may need it in the future.

For the most part, one major difference between being a hoe and someone who is trafficked is having ownership of one's body. The most important term within the previous statement is "ownership". For a person to have ownership of their body means they have full autonomy or control of their body to do whatever they desire to do. For example, if they want a haircut, they will get one. If they want to get a tattoo, they will get it. If they want to have sex with two people, they will do it because it is their desire to do so. Those who possess ownership of their body often project the same traits on to others who do not have that privilege. Just to double back on that statement for those who missed the message; it is a privilege to have ownership of your body. To understand this privilege more, think about the difference between someone at age 17 to someone at age 18. Before 18, it is all about parental consent.

Ownership of oneself can easily be taken from a person, especially if that person is underage. As an example, let's review our discussion on sexual violence. For some survivors of sexual violence, if the survivor was a virgin when they were assaulted, the perpetrator often has ownership of the survivor because the perpetrator took a choice from them. I have been in a similar situation in my life. Something that helped me claim my ownership back from my perpetrators was to change my concept of virginity. I chose to define my virginity as being something that could not be taken but only given away with my consent, and this consent must be respected throughout the encounter. Under the old definition, I lost my virginity as a 2-year-old. Under my definition, I lost my virginity at the age of 19 and I am proud of it because it was my choice.

Having ownership of one's body is empowering. It allows you the ability to heal and work within your own best interest. You are not living your life for the approval of others. You are living your life for yourself. Additionally, you are living your life in such a way that it inspires others to have ownership of themselves as well. Having ownership of oneself is simply having the ability to be free within any circumstance. Having ownership of your body will make you a better lover, a better friend, a better parent, and a better role model. However, having ownership of oneself requires work and self-reflection. But that will be a discussion for a later chapter.

With all the positivity around the greatness that comes with owning your body, I will be remiss if I do not highlight the most important difference between the hoe and prostitute once more. A hoe has ownership of their own body, however, a prostitute does not. A prostitute is considered the property of their pimp or oppressor.

Keep in mind that a pimp no longer looks like the crowd of a Dave Chappelle skit or the infamous A Pimp Named Slickback. A pimp has a degree behind their name. They are parents. They are professionals. They are influencers and motivators. Pimps and other human traffickers are even people with authority and power like judges and police officers. They are anyone looking to exploit those who are vulnerable for money.

Based on the last statements, some may begin to suggest, "well if a pimp can be all of that, am I being pimped out every time I show up for work?" I understand why some may think that, but remember, this generalization is to show how broad pimping has become in terms of human trafficking and to tie in how the average person you may think is not a pimp may actually be a pimp. For example, your neighbor may be a pimp; well, a better term will be *human trafficker*. This is not to insight fear, but to educate. The scope of a human trafficker is as broad as the scope of those who fall victim.

There is a difference between a person who chooses to have sex for money and those who are forced into having sex in exchange for money and *security*. A human trafficker often displays their ownership of their victim by becoming their source of security in every level. They become their victims' source of financial security, food, social engagement, work-life (or lack of life) balance, health, addiction management, affirmation, confidence, and validation. Essentially, the human trafficker holds all aspects of their victims' lives. Many survivors and current survivors in the making have been told who they are going to sleep with and are punished when their earnings are not up to par.

I invite the reader to join me in a mental journey. This journey is about love and satisfaction. This is one of those memories that is accompanied by warm scents. Think about the wafting scent of vanilla, honey, and a small hint of cinnamon. Think about the pleasant smell of perfectly baked, homemade cookies. The aroma so tantalizing that it causes your body to shiver. That is the mindset that is needed to join me on this mental journey. If you are not there yet, hopefully you will be there soon.

Imagine, if you will, to a time where you are at your prime and able to enjoy any aspect of your life. There has been heart break in your life, but you are moving past it. You want to be happy. You also want your perfect mate. One day you decide that you are going to make improvements in your life and decide to go to your favorite store for some retail therapy. Soon after making your purchases for the day, you begin your trip back home when you run into an old friend. You have not thought about them in years, but the only thought you have about them now is how much they have changed.

This person is pleasing to your eyes. They are your type. They are the definition of sexiness. As you gaze upon them, you admire their physique. You think about all the things you would rather do with them behind closed doors if you had the chance. I will let you sit in that idea for a while. Let your imagination go wild in the sexual possibilities. From slow caresses to rough sex. From foot rubbing to sexual massages. From discussing possibilities to having deep and intimate conversations. You see a world of happiness and pleasure. You finally snap back into reality when they ask how you have been.

You respond to them letting them know that you have been fine. Life is alright and you are just finding your purpose or something random because you do not really want to be 100% truthful with them. Rather than leaving the conversation, the person mentions they used to have strong feelings for you and asks if you are single. You respond honestly and say yes. The person then tells you that it must be their lucky day, or it must be a fated encounter. They ask you if you would be interested in going out some time. This is where the plot thickens, you tell them no. You tell them that you have a lot on your plate and getting into a relationship right now seems like too much stress. Rather than pushing the topic, the person says it was worth it to ask you no matter the response, but they are happy they had the chance to see you again.

A couple of months pass. By yet another strange coincidence, you run into this person again. They have been on your mind and they look even better this time. This time, you become bold and ask them if they are still available for a date. They coyishly respond saying they do not know. They then smile and say yes. The two of you begin laughing. You enjoy this person's sense of humor. Their smile makes you feel warm. Their presence is filling. They are a joy to be around.

You are now in an established relationship with this person. For the sake of this story going forward, I will refer to them as your partner. You and your partner have had a wonderful time enjoying each other's company for the last 6 months. During this timeframe, you have mentioned your dreams of an ideal family. You talk about your ideal job and home. You begin to see how well your life and their life intertwine. Your partner is the one for you. They love you and you love them, regardless of the amount of time you have been together. You can tell this person is the one you have been wanting for a long time. The communication is perfect, and the sex is immaculate. To make it better, this person caters to your every desire.

Before long, you and your partner begin talking about the future of your relationship and living together. Your partner then tells you they actually have enough space at their place for up to 3 extra people. They extend an invitation to move in. They say it is not mandatory, but if you feel the need to move in, the offer is always open. Your partner adds on to the offer by highlighting one of your goals of going back to school to further your education. They say you can go back to school if you want to and you do not have to worry about paying for rent. Your partner even offers to assist you in paying for school, if the need presents itself. You agree to move in and work on your applications together.

After a few months of living together, you realize your partner has become less involved. This does not seem like them because the two of you are able to talk about anything with each other. Your partner tells you that they are agitated because one of their friends left drugs in their car. You tell your partner to get rid of it because you do not want them to be punished for their friend's mistake. Your partner tells you that there is up to $4,000 worth of drugs that was left and your partner does not have that much cash laying around to cover the cost if and when the friend notices they left the drugs behind. You mention to your partner the only other way to get rid of the drugs other than turning it over to the police or flushing it will be returning the drugs to the friend.

They respond by saying they do not trust their friend to come to the house because of the people the friend associates with. Your partner also says their vehicle will be easy to point out in the neighborhood the friend resides in, therefore, dropping it off is out of the question. They then ask you if you are comfortable enough with giving the drugs back to the friend in a safe place where no one will notice. There is some tension in the room. The partner then double downs on reassuring your safety. They reassure you that no one will recognize what is going on. You agree to do it.

The swapping of the drugs went off without anyone noticing a thing, as your partner promised. The friend apologized many times and offered to pay you for the inconvenience. You accept the money which they handed to you in a pouch. When you return home, your partner is there. You tell them of the encounter and tell them about the money the friend gave you. You sit down to count the money and see that the friend gave you $8,000. You share the news with your partner, and they are shocked. Your partner suggests to you to give them $6,000; $4,000 will be stored at the bank and saved for your educational pursuit and the remainder will go to the house fund for emergencies. The rest of the money was for you to spend it on everything that makes you happy. Your partner seems to be back to normal.

You have fully settled down into your new environment. During the last few months, you have turned away from much of your family and friends. Your partner highlights how they rarely reach out to you and that they must be jealous of your happiness. While preparing to go back to school, you make the choice to cut back on work in order to focus more on your education. Because of the emergency fund, you have enough money to support yourself for some time. Also, your partner has been really supportive. You have grown accustomed to your partner leaving small tokens of appreciation around the house and the occasional $300 with a note encouraging you to get something special for yourself. In a sense, your partner has become your main source of joy.

One day, there is an unexpected flood in your home. Your partner tells you everything is fine. Unfortunately, your partner did not have flood insurance; therefore, the repairs will be an out of pocket expense. A contractor comes to the home and advises you and your partner that it may take a month for the proper repairs to be made but may take longer depending on if there is damage to the home's foundation. Your partner assures you that they have the majority of the expenses covered and asks that you pay roughly $3,000 and book a nice hotel. Your partner says it is obviously time for the two of you to go on a much-needed vacation with each other. The room however will have to be paid out of your pocket.

Your partner gives you a list of 3 luxury hotels; all are less than an hour's drive away from the home. You attempt to book a room for 30 days and see that the total is close to $10,000. You then inform your partner that if the total amount came from your pockets, you will overdraft your account. Your partner suggest that you pay up to your limit and they will cover the rest. They also say, because of the inconvenience, they will give you a daily allowance just to make sure you enjoy the vacation in full, but to be safe, they will have to get a prepaid card to prevent overspending on the trip. You agree and the two of you head to your luxury vacation.

The first night in the hotel is a night to remember. The two of you make passionate love. You are at peace. You are joyous. The next morning, you want to go to a restaurant next to the hotel for brunch. You remember that you have no available funds in your account and ask your partner for the purchase card. Your partner apologizes and jokingly say they will not give you the card until you give them a kiss. You give them a loving kiss and like magic, the card is in your hand. You take the card and head to the restaurant. At the restaurant you decide to order bottomless mimosas with the daily special. On this day, the special is called Sun and Moon. The waiter says, "The name is an artistic representation of the phases of life. The meal starts out with a bowl of squash puree with caviar strategically placed in the center of the bowl atop a fresh and crispy cracker. This will be accompanied by our house special smoked salmon which sits on a bed of romaine lettuce, shredded carrots, and cherry tomatoes, lightly served, of course, with a generous drizzle of our special balsamic rose vinaigrette. We call it that because we soak our garlic cloves in rose water over night, so our balsamic rose vinaigrette is able to provide each guest with a sweet kiss of romance in every bite".

You enjoy your meal. You are given your check and see the meal is $65.42. You give the waiter your prepaid card. They return to the table and inform you the card has been declined due to insufficient funds. You contact your partner and tell them of the mishap. Your partner sounds frustrated because the card has $50 on it due to budget constraints as a result of having to pay for the home repairs. You become apologetic. Your partner says, its fine but be smarter next time. Your partner also says they do not know what you are going to do for dinner or other meals during the day. You are hurt by the statement. You feel guilty for putting your partner in the current predicament. Shortly after your conversation, your partner arrives to the restaurant and pays the full balance.

On your way back to the hotel, you apologize to your partner once more. They tell you it is fine. Your partner says they decided to pay the balance because they will rather sacrifice their meals for the day to make sure you are able to enjoy a more affordable meal in the future. Later that day, you and your partner have another round of passionate love making. Afterward, your partner says they are willing to sacrifice a little bit more of their budget so the two of you can order a filling meal off the room service menu. Your partner uploads an additional $50 to the prepaid card. Your partner then places an order and pays for the meal using the prepaid card.

The next week is an adjustment for you, but you become accustomed to living within your $50 budget. You mostly stay in the room to keep yourself from overspending by utilizing the variety of luxury services provided by the hotel. Your partner tends to come and go as they please. Your partner mentions they are looking into new investments opportunities within the city and your mind is more focused on relaxation instead of business ventures. When your partner comes back to the hotel early in the afternoon, they suggest spicing up the sexual relationship by adding a third person. Your partner says it does not have to be ongoing, but they want to give it a try and think you both will like it. They even suggest that the third person can be a person of any gender. Your partner says they are just interested in enjoying the experience with you. You feel as though you owe it to your partner to do something nice for them.

You and your partner agree to find someone together. You and your partner start your search in the bar of the hotel. Your partner points at a few people and asks, "What about them?" You scratch a number of people off of your mental list and finally decide to attempt to have the threesome with a person sitting at the end of the bar. Your partner goes over to them and sparks up the conversation. Before leaving, your partner suggests that it will be best if only one person goes to propose the idea in order to keep from intimidating the person. Both the patron and your pimp look over to you and smile.

Later in the evening, there is a knock at the door. Your partner goes to greet the guest. You are comfortably lying on the bed, waiting for the two of them to enter into the room. Your partner and the person enter into the bedroom, your pimp has a bottle of champagne in one hand and three flutes. Your pimp begins to undress. You begin to follow suit and so does the third-party participant. For the purposes of this story, let's refer to them as Jay. Jay begins to kiss around your neck while your partner begins to perform oral sex. Jay kisses you down the left side of your body and assists your pimp in performing oral sex on you. Your partner then kisses their way up your body. Their kisses stop at the tip of your nipple. Your pimp's sweet kisses become passionate licks around the tip of your nipple and circles the outline of your areola. Your partner delivers passionate kisses, licks, bites, and sucks meanwhile Jay is catering to every need and desire of your groin. The passion continues until the late hours of the evening until you have climaxed at least three times.

When you wake up the next morning, you notice there is a roughly $100 left on the counter. You wake to see a text from your pimp saying they really enjoyed themselves last night and Jay enjoyed I, too. I am just going to stop this story at this point. For some, this is their reality as they are eased into prostitution. They are presented with a beautiful dream life just to have that life stripped from them. If I were to continue this tale, there will be a retelling of how deeply indebted the newly recruited prostitute, in this case, you, the reader, has become to your pimp. I will have to shine light on how the pimp deleted messages from your phone while you were not paying attention in order to show that your family does not reach out to you. I will have to shine the light on how much your pimp has twisted your reality in such a way to make you believe that your family is not looking out for your best interest in life because they are jealous. I might even have to highlight that each incident from the flood in the home to the contractor to making you spend all your savings to being at a bar is all within your pimp's guide for recruiting you. I will have to highlight that the pimp has multiple recordings of you in compromising positions, like delivering drugs to a drug dealer they do business with on a regular basis. I might even have to be sure to mention how your pimp was able to clock you as a potential prostitute before your first surprise meeting. But what I have highlighted is one of the many possible roads to becoming a victim of sex trafficking.

Also, keep in mind that sex trafficking affects our youth. Within the United States, sex trafficking affects our youth within the foster care system at a disproportionate rate. This also affects young adult and teen runaways. I want to share a not so proud moment in my life with you all. Within this incident, I cannot make a claim on the individual's circumstances, but I do take ownership in failing someone who needed assistance.

One evening, I was at a Waffle House enjoying a great conversation with the staff members. This was a month after the Nashville Waffle House shooting in 2018. Granted, I was not in Nashville, but this was a time where mass shootings were happening on a regular basis (essentially any year prior to COVID-19 – where the shootings continued for a targeted minority population with the same lack of accountability towards the murderers; for the sake of this example, let us call them police and white Americans). We will come back to them later, I promise. Now, back to the story.

While sitting inside, a young boy came into the restaurant carrying a bookbag. For those who are already at the realization of where this is going, remember, I acknowledge I failed to act. For those who are not there yet, I just want to highlight that there was fear in the restaurant. We did not know if there was going to be another repeat of the Nashville shooting. The boy then sat down, and all eyes were on him. He asked if anyone has a phone charger. Unfortunately, no one within the restaurant had one to offer. I would like to add, when he asked, my mind immediately went to the Dylann Roof incident in South Carolina.

Shortly after everyone mentioned they did not have a charger; the boy left the restaurant. A few of the staff members let out a sigh of relief and one of the patrons made a reference that they believed this was going to be the next waffle house on the news. After a few minutes passed and I gained a peace of mind, I realized the boy was homeless and needed help. Each person that was present had failed this child for not taking action and for not asking if he were ok. We failed him by not helping him find safe resources that will benefit him. We allowed our anxiety, for some, past traumas, prevent us from taking action. Though our fears were justified based upon recent events of the time, it is no excuse for our failure. This is partly why the cliché "when you know better, you do better" exists. It is time for us all to better.

As we are, we live in a society where legal loopholes exists in order to safeguard human trafficking. We also live in a society where prostitutes are penalized for their sexual labor, yet many of their buyers are not. Additionally, there have been a multitude of cover-ups involving police officers and sex trafficking which includes the purchasing of prostitutes, sexual abuse of the prostitutes—with some being underage—and physical and emotional abuse of prostitutes. But for some out there, this is okay because that behavior is what prostitutes deserve. For those who think this is what their fellow human beings deserve, seek help. No one deserves to be treated in this manner. If you do not believe so, why is it that there is so much offense taken when a person is likened to a whore, a prostitute, or a slur? Because being called such a term is akin to being called less than human.

In a perfect world, well, in a world where there was proper training of our police force and utilizations of national, statewide, and citywide resources, there will be safe havens for those wishing to escape being trafficked or those who are discovered as a victim. Let me paint a picture of what I would love to see.

First, I want to see a police force that represents the community it is sworn to protect. When I say represents, I mean the officers come from the community, they are more diverse than the community, and receive ongoing education and training that both development the officer professionally and keeps them abreast on the ever-changing demographics of their community. By being more diverse than the community, I am referring to diversity in a sense of race, color, religion, national origin, sex, physical or mental disability, or age. I am looking for the true definition of an equal opportunity employer. I will love to see officers who are trained well enough to provide assistance to individuals in need of help that can only communicate through sign language. Officers who are trained to negotiate before resulting to violence. I will love to see officers treat every person as though they matter and deserve redemption. As it stands, I would rather have a precinct of collegiate level resident assistants (RA) over our current police. You know what, what if every officer is required to go through RA training?

It is a funny thought, but to those who do not know what the typical RA learns during training, here is a brief overview. First and foremost, they learn how to build rapport within their community. Of course, there is the programming aspect of the job, but that will not be the main takeaways here; however, that will better relationships with the community. The typical RA is encouraged to be seen and be available to their community regardless if there is an incident or not. They are encouraged to know the names of each person within their community. The typical RA is encouraged to be a resource to their residents in case their residents have an issue with roommates or other individuals within the community. The typical RA is also encouraged to be a listening ear when their residents come to them just to talk. Ras are also required to seek assistance from professional staff workers when the situation calls for back up or a specific service such as counseling, police issues, or medical emergencies. The typical RA is also trained in de-escalation, conflict management, and breaking up unsanctioned parties on campus.

If you know of any Ras, please reach out to them and give them a hug, if after the pandemic, or just give them warm words of encouragement with a thank you. They deserve it. Ras do a lot. Ras and other housing professionals are often the first responders of incidents on campus and, depending on the campus, the situation is under control by the time campus police arrive to the scene. This is not to say that campus police or the off-campus precincts are unable to handle a situation, but their presence often adds more aggression to a situation rather than a calming feel. Much of this anxiety built around police officers is due to a history of unchecked brutality and the abuse of power. Some of the unchecked brutality includes unarmed shootings, sexual harassment, spousal abuse, sexual violence, coercion, and threats to do harm at the expense of refusing to comply. I am amazed at how many television shows exists that highlight many of the atrocities within our criminal justice system, yet people deny there is a problem. But that is a discussion for another day.

I hope the day comes soon where drug abusers are pointed toward services that will assist them in fighting their addiction. I dream of a society where mental health professionals and social workers are called to the scene of a domestic disputes to ensure the victims have someone to help them process their traumatic experience. Additionally, I will love to see programs geared towards helping repeat offenders and others who are incarcerated process traumatic experiences from their past or those obtained since becoming incarcerated. I wish for the day where the focus of our criminal justice system is more focused on reform and properly preparing inmates on adjusting to life outside of prison with a list of services that will assist in easing the transition rather than focus on the amount of profit that can be made from using next to free labor. I envision the day where sex work is legal and does not allow for abusers to continue to operate without proper consequences. I dream of the day where we all have ownership of our bodies. It is all possible, we just have to be willing to do the necessary work.

Just a reminder to all readers, if you are looking to live the life of the hoe, well the life defined within this text, part of that life requires paying homage and respect to those who hold the title of prostitute. It is unfortunate that there has been an insurmountable number of victims of prostitution who have been brutalized over the years. To those who are survivors, I am sorry for all that you have experienced. I am also thankful and appreciative of the stories you all have shared that have fueled many of the champions against sex tracking. Human trafficking is thriving within the United States and other countries. It is a sad truth, but it is a truth, nonetheless. Human trafficking affects its victims both physically and mentally. For any person who wants to learn more about human trafficking, I encourage you to visit the Department of Health and Human Services website. Additionally, look into some documentaries and TED Talks. There is so much information available to us, we just have to be open to learning and listening. Remaining ignorant is just as active as learning new information. Remember, when you know better you do better. If there must be one lesson learned from 2020, the lesson is ignorance is a choice. Take that however you wish. I said what I said.

Resources

National Human Trafficking Hotline
- https://humantraffickinghotline.org/
- 888-373-7888 (TTY: 711)
- Text HELP to 233733
- Email at help@humantraffickinghotline.org
- One may use any of these options to report a tip as well

National Domestic Violence Hotline
- https://www.thehotline.org/
- 800-799-SAFE (7233)
- TTY: 800-787-3224

Department of Health & Human Services Office on Trafficking in Persons
- https://www.acf.hhs.gov/otip
- https://www.acf.hhs.gov/otip/about/myths-facts-human-trafficking

https://www.acf.hhs.gov/otip/partnerships/look-beneath-the-surface

Slaytor Jackston

Chapter 4

Safety is a Priority

When one brings up safety within the context of sex, the common thought is either condoms or the pill. Over the years, there has been an increase in awareness around different birth control methods and condom usage. I am happy to see this; however, I have noticed that there is a trend of people not wanting to use protection during sexual encounters. I would love to say that this chapter is going to be geared towards discussing all of the different contraceptives out there, but I am not. As I mentioned before, there's a multitude of awareness about them and I would rather keep this chapter brief. I will, however, discuss ways of staying safe.

In addition to wearing condoms when having sex with multiple partners, please get tested on a regular basis. I will forever encourage people to get tested because there are too many diseases spreading in this world, many of which can be avoided. Though some diseases have cures, there are also those that do not have a cure. If there is anything that you can do to reduce the risk of spreading diseases, I recommend doing it and utilizing testing options. Some of the sexually transmitted infections are able to do a lot more damage to your body if not caught on time, regardless of gender expression.

With testing comes honest communication. I am not telling you to disclose your status immediately. If you are not comfortable enough with the person to disclose your status, I will recommend not engaging in sex with the person until you trust them enough to tell them or utilize some form of barrier method. This is not me telling anyone what to do with their body, but reminding you to ensure you are being respectful of your partner(s)'s body. Also, do not indicate that you are free of any sexual diseases if you have not been tested. Regardless if you only do oral, frottage, or whatever else falls within your sexual behavior, know your status. Knowing your status is a benefit for you and your partner(s). You may even get tested with your partner(s).

If your results are positive for any sexual infection, the best practice is to notify those you have been sexually intimate with. There is pain in hearing this news and there is fear attached with those positive results. The hurt and fear is understandable. First and foremost, feel what you need to feel and then seek out whatever resource you need that will assist you with overcoming the news. Those who you notify may lash out or reject the news. Some may flat out say you did not get the disease from them. Some may even appreciate you for letting them know. People react differently; it is hard to know how anyone will react to such news. Regardless of the reaction, I want you to focus on yourself because your pain is just as valid as the other person's.

Positive results have a stigma attached to them. For example, some indicate that they are free of sexual diseases by saying they are "clean", implying that those with a disease are dirty. Having a disease does not make a person dirty. Clean is just another one of the many microaggressions that exist in this world. Those who test positive for any disease, be it in the past or ongoing, are still sexual beings worthy of love and affection.

Other than sexual safety, one also must think about physical safety. There are dangers out there, some of which have been discussed in previous chapters. I wish I could say there are no dangers out there, but there are many people who prey on the weak and attack the strong. To keep myself from telling adults how to be responsible, I will keep this short. If you feel unsafe, let someone know. When traveling, be sure to tell others you trust where you are going. Share your GPS location with those you trust. Communicate your actions while out on the town and send pictures of people and places, if need be. Whatever you need to make sure you feel safe, I say do it.

Chapter 5

This is Not *the Game*

This statement is a bit problematic, but I take ownership of what I am about to say. I love Kelly Price's song "Friend of Mine" feat. Ronald Isley and R. Kelly. I know, I am trash. But I am human, and the song is a guilty pleasure. I mention this song because of Ron Isley's verse referring to knowing *the game*. I do not know too many people who have not been impacted by *the game*; be it a willing player or unwilling. Personally, I was never a fan of *the game* even though I have been told so much about it growing up. You play *the game* and not let *the game* play you. The lessons just never really stuck with me.

The game allows a person to make their sexual partners into a pawn on the chess board, a tic mark, or even a mission. A few personal examples that I have encountered of people who made missions out of playing *the game*: 1) wanting to scratch sex with a black guy off their sex list; 2) wanting to *score* with 5 people within a 24 hour time frame and see which friend completes the task first; 3) just want to see what birthday sex is like.

Let me start by saying I am not an expert in *the game*, nor do I wish to be. If that's your doctrine and practice, good for you. But I will relay what I have gathered from "teachings" and highlight the difference between hoeing and playing the proverbial game. Over the years, I began to separate myself from the mentality that practices *the game*. I took on a position of observing the behaviors of others as they used *the game* within their relationships. From what I gathered, *the game* is for children and not growing adults. *The game* looked as though it was an ongoing circle of emotional hurt, trauma, and deceit. It was not and is not appealing.

When I reflect on how *the game* has been played for so many years, I am shocked how there has been no means of improving a failed system. Actually, I take that back. There are those who are able to keep their business discreet when playing *the game*, a good portion of them being women. Granted, the way *the game* is played changed when cellphones became a thing. In my opinion, *the game* is a major contributing factor to the tic-for-tac relationship found in some couples—when their partner does wrong, they do something equally or more wrong as retribution. At the end of the day, *the game* is a contributing factor of a lot of childish behavior of supposed adults.

Have you ever heard of the term "scoring"? This term is not referring to scoring points playing a sport or video game. This term refers to sexual conquest where the only time a person gets a point is by catching a body. I am not going to break down the last portion of that statement. If you do not know, then, oh well. I can travel down the rabbit hole of how negative the term "scoring" is when it comes to rape culture and what not, but I think by this point we all have a general understanding of consent and the horrors of rape. If not, please go back to Chapter 2.

The term "scoring" gamifies sexuality and sexual encounters. It provides a point value that does not fully equate to the full value of a person and their self-worth. They are turned into just another body that was sexualized.

Let it be stated that my distaste for *the game* does not come from a place of hurt, but from a desire for honesty within communicating one's intentions. There are many people who have developed deep rooted insecurities and trust issues as a result from being played. Some people have been played out of money, house and home, security, or love. From my objective view of *the game*, it only brings issues for both the player and those getting played. From what I have seen thus far, those who play *the game* have some of the most severe case of trust issues because they believe their partner is doing the same thing they are doing or were doing in the past.

I am a firm believer of karma, but I do not think it is always a physical manifestation. We get what we put out into this world. If we sow the seeds of distrust throughout our lives, those seeds will bloom in a form of action or mental distress. Think about it. How many times have you seen a person push away a partner who loves them unconditionally? Or, you may have been that partner that was pushed away. The person allows their insecurities to make their false perceptions into a reality. For example, Paternity Court. I am a fan of the show and the healing Lauren Lake brings to families. Many times, I have seen an episode where a partner projects their insecurities on their significant other that it drives them to cheat or they remain faithful and end the relationship after truths have been revealed. Granted, this is not always the case, but this is just one of the many results that happens as a result of reaping what one sows

Because of the negative connotation that often comes with the phrase "reaping what one sows", it would be remiss of me to not make a disclaimer. Reaping comes in different forms. Sometimes it can be something that negatively impacts a person, such as a break-up. Reaping can also mean having ownership of your actions and holding yourself accountable for your actions. Reaping can also mean exhibiting growth. There are many ways one may be able to reap whatever they have sown; the difference is based on choice to change what seeds you are planting or keeping the old strategy.

The major difference between *the game* and hoeing is practicing honesty. There are no pretenses, just intentionality. What are your intentions? Let it be known. There are no "take the hints". There is clear rejection and clear intent. Now, I know there are some justifiable arguments for the "take the hint" approach, but that argument remains justifiable because we have fostered a culture where rejection is damaging. My argument towards that is making rejection a normal part of life. If people can handle rejection from a job, they should be able to handle rejection on other levels as well. If you are a person that cannot handle rejection, I recommend working on yourself before attempting dating, hoeing, or any situation that calls for establishing interpersonal relationships. It is a hard truth that must be absorbed.

One positive attribute of playing *the game* is the ability to move on to the next potential relationship. At times, we will face rejection. That is okay. As the saying goes, there are plenty of fish in the sea. Now, I think of that saying in a different way than others. I have been told when I catch a fish and it ends up not working in my favor, I should put them back and try again for another fish. The advice is useful, but I do not like it. Rather than letting that fish go, I choose to let the fish remain in my boat, so I do not leave myself open to catching that same fish in the future. Now, this is not saying I harbor feelings for the person that has rejected me. However, this is a way for me to acknowledge what is not for me. Those that are released back into the sea are those that either may be the perfect match for me after they have grown more – be it mentally, fiscally, or emotionally.

The ability to move on to the next potential relationship is often seen when a person is playing the field. When playing *the game*, playing the field is often defined as having multiple suitors who believe they are the only person you are involved with. Sometimes, this includes an outside party knowing they are not the only person you, the individual, is involved with, yet someone within the entanglement is left unaware. Somewhere within the realm of playing the field, someone is being lied to. Playing *the game* and playing the field thrives in ambiguity. There are no set boundaries and no establishment of where all parties stand within the relationship. The only thing that is established are hopes and dreams without concrete actions. Playing the field is riddled with potential drama and cover ups. Playing the field is anxiety driven and becomes a recipe for disaster.

One way to demystify the ambiguity is to set a clear understanding of terms, phrases, and actions. One of the most common terms used in today's society geared towards defining a relationship is saying that you are "talking" to someone. As a caveat, I know what I say does not dictate how a person should live their life; but, there is some use for what I am saying, nonetheless. If you and another person are "just talking" you are not in a romantic relationship. How you define talking is up to you. It may involve sex, it may not. However, at the end of the day, the romantic relationship is not established until both parties are on the same page.

Now, let us move toward the term dating. Think about dating as the early phases of creating a contract. You are getting to know more about your partner within the romantic relationship and they do the same towards you. Notice, I said romantic relationship. I use this wording to highlight that the relationship is established as a romantic relationship. When dating someone, it is up to those within the relationship to discuss what is allowed and what is not allowed. For example, it is perfectly fine for someone to date more than one person. It is also okay and valid to be dating monogamously. There is no set standard on how a person should date, it is up to the individuals. If, however, those wishing to date each other do not agree with the same form of dating, why continue to be in a romantic relationship with each other? This does not necessarily mean you cannot continue talking to them or whatever the relationship consisted of prior to seeking an established romantic relationship. However, I suggest using this as an opportunity to look elsewhere for someone who wishes to establish a mutually agreeable version of a romantic relationship.

Now, let us talk about titles. Boyfriend. Girlfriend. Partner. Bae. Boo. Significant other. Husband. Wife. Spouse. Fiancé. Fiancée. Fuck buddy. There are just so many titles. Some are contractual and some are given just to show progression. No matter what the title may be, the one thing I do know about a title is the ability for it to be changed or taken away. In a sense, a title means nothing if you are not going to put in the necessary work towards the relationship. Personally, I do not like pet names. I need my partner(s) to know me by name. Just a pro tip, those pet names are the easiest way to exist in the realm of ambiguity.

I mention titles to highlight one thing. Just because you have a title or the relationship is established as a romantic relationship, it does not mean there will not be obstacles or doubt that may come along. People come into relationships with baggage and this baggage must be unpacked and laid to rest. I am not going to spend much time talking on the subject because this is not the book for relationship advice. Now, if the readers want something like that, feel free to let me know. Jokes aside, I have seen people play *the game* and convince others they are the one just to leave them high and dry after sex or at the first sign of trouble. This is partly why ghosting is such a big thing. Now, I would not say ghosting was birthed from playing *the game*, however, it does exist within the culture of hitting *it* and quitting. Some ghosting is due to valid reason and failure in knowing how to communicate, and some incidents of ghosting are due to falling in love with possibilities and potential and realizing later down the line you have made a mistake. Whatever the case may be, ghosting sometimes happen but playing *the game* still remains akin to childish behavior within the adult world.

There is a sense of maturity that must come with acting like a hoe or living your best hoe life (more to come on this subject in a future chapter). There is no room for games when there's a possibility of a life altering event caused by sex. This can be catching a sexually transmitted infection or becoming a co-parent with someone you do not want to raise a child with. There is no gray area when it comes to being a hoe. Relationships must be defined and mutually agreed upon. As multiple chapters have indicated thus far, consent is needed and ideal. No matter what, remind yourself of the cliché of there being plenty of fish out there for you to catch. Some may be harder than others, but the fish you want and desire is out there. With there being more people becoming more open about their sexuality, the need to lie about your intent in engaging with them becomes less warranted.

I want to take this opportunity to bring up the topic of those who are on the down-low (DL). There are plenty of misconceptions that exist about those on the DL. One of those misconceptions is that the person is just gay, are bisexual, or has HIV/AIDS. There's a lot but these are three I have heard most often. Those that are DL do not often fall under this category. I bring this topic up because some incorporate the lifestyle of being DL with playing *the game* when that is not always the case.

Some have confused DL with being discreet. Being discreet is choosing to not have your business open to the public. Not because you fear exposure, but because the only business the individual cares about is their business and people often times want to mind businesses that have paid them nary a penny nor a pissing pot.

Now, this does not discredit those who are on the DL for stability and safety reasons. I mention this because I do not understand why people choose to out others. We do not know the circumstances another individual is facing at home or within their family. Now, this is not me justifying cheating in any way, that is a different scenario. Some individuals who are on the DL are single. Many of the people I have talked to in the past, be it romantic or conversationally, were single but fearful of losing friends and family. Some were fearful of dying as a result of backlash. Some have committed suicide from being outed. The decision to come out, no matter the person's sexual orientation or gender expression, belongs to the individual—not an outside party.

Outside of these individuals, there are, believe it or not, some people on the DL that seek pleasure from strangers solely because they are too afraid to speak about their sexual desires to their partners out of fear the relationship may end. For example, I have had talks with heterosexual men who hate having sex with other men and penis owners but do so because they do not know how to ask their partner to try pegging. They also fear their partner will think they are gay. If you do not know this already, let me say this for you now: a person is not gay if they want to be pleased anally. It is just another sexual activity that provides stimulation and pleasure to your partner. The same can be said when it comes to cunnilingus. An individual is not less of a man if they so choose to perform oral sex on a partner who happens to have a vagina. I guess I might as well add the same terms applies to oral sex that involves the anus. Overall, it is best to separate sexual orientation from sexual acts. Those are two separate entities.

Back to the topic of those who are on the DL. Yes, there is the possibility of the person being bisexual and in the closet about their attraction to the same sex, however, there are many people who are bisexual and can have a monogamist relationship with someone regardless of their gender or gender expression (for those who identify as pansexual). A person who chooses to be on the DL with the sole purpose of cheating on their partner is cheating because they are a cheater, not because they are on the DL. There is a clear difference among the two. No matter whom the DL individual is cheating with, they are cheating.

In this light, the designation of DL is a guise which allows them to remain anonymous and out of sight from those who may alert their partner of the cheating. Some are bold and cheat in the open. Others may use a common phrase such as "someone stole my pics and made an account trying to ruin what we have together". Sometimes that is the truth; but, many times, it is a lie. Only you know your partner; however, I am a firm believer that actions speak louder than words.

For those who use the guise of DL in a way to continue to play *the game*, I have no sympathy or empathy for you when your crops come due. I just hope there is changed behavior and growth. For those who are reading and truly feel unsafe with who you are, I send positive vibes and love your way in hopes one day you can live your best, happy and authentic life. For those who have hopes of outing a particular person, remember the message about reaping what you sow. I wish no negativity upon you, but I wish for growth. From what I have seen in the past, those who out others do so from a place of hurt. I just hope you get to a place where you are able to let the hurt go.

I am the furthest from a fan of playing *the game*. I have seen it ruin families and dissolve trust. I have seen it set a standard of hurting innocent people who were not the cause of the player's pain and make those bystanders become bearers of that hurt and, in turn, hurt others; creating a cycle. *The game* has established a toxic culture. A culture that tells young men that they should start having sex at an early age. A culture that has taught women that it is okay to allow a person to pressure or persuade them into having sex when they are not in the mood.

The game and its teachings have taught young people that alcohol and drugs are tools to enhance one's probability of *scoring* and increase their pleasure when it is actually more numbing. It has fostered a culture where feelings no longer matter and becomes a thing meant to be toyed with. *The game* has developed a culture where a high body count becomes a qualifier for a trophy or reward, even though body count does not define a person's success or their identity as a human and sexual being. Based on the amount of lives that were negatively impacted in the past and present, I would argue that *the game* is just a failed system, and I wish it never existed. Essentially, *the game* is a false sense of superiority played by adult children who fail to see they are participating in inappropriate and dishonest behavior. Those who play it lack the skills to hold themselves accountable for their actions and the potential outcomes. If you are hurt by this statement, I said what I muthafucking said.

Chapter 6

Judgement and Sexual Positivity

I have lived much of my life with a positive mindset when it pertains to sexuality. This is not to say that I did not have issues with coming into my identity; but, overall, I disliked double standards—especially when it came to sex. I was told body count does not matter, but a woman should remain a virgin. I was also told that it is okay to have sex before marriage, but a woman should hold off until their wedding night. It did not make sense to me. *If I am not having sex with other men, who am I to be having sex with before marriage?*

Double standards are excuses used to find justification for sexual oppression and oppression in other avenues. In an age of birth control, ovulation tracking apps, and science, what is the purpose for these double standards?

I am not going to get on my soap box in this chapter because there is much more to sexual positivity than living outside of the realm of double standards. Sexual positivity has been around for more than 90 years. I would even say sexual positivity is ancient. Arguably, sexual positivity existed as a norm until restrictions on sexual activity became religious and law. Now, when I mention sexual positivity, I am only talking about consenting adults. This book, and me as an individual, does not support sexual intercourse between an adult and a child. Though historical documents may suggest support of such things, we are in a different age where life expectancy is not an average of 37 years or younger. Seek help because you are not healthy.

Evidence of having multiple sex partners, sexual partners of the same sex, or partners that are gender fluid can be found in multiple cultures. Additionally, there are texts—such as the Kama Sutra—that are dedicated to teaching the art of pleasurable sex. Sexual positivity has been around for years, however, when it comes to oppression—or simply having power over others—positive sexuality seems new.

In recent years, I have seen many people associate living their best life with exploring their sexuality to its fullest. I am not going to take away from them in that aspect, but I also do not subscribe to that narrative. Essentially, I feel as though living your best life is living life as your authentic self while making the necessary changes that will allow you to live your life free of worry that may stem from sex, finances, personal relationships, and lack of control over one's time and surroundings. Like I mentioned in the previous chapter, if one is exploring their sexuality to its fullest, they are living their best hoe life and I am all for it.

I will be going more in detail about living the life of the hoe in the next chapter. This chapter is more based on much of the insecurities that people often face when it comes to expressing their sexuality, some of which were discussed in Chapter 5. Again, there is not a one-fits-all approach to dealing with insecurities or expressing one's sexuality. Think of sexual expression as having your hands full of sand while on a beach. Five hundred people can go to the same beach and walk away with a different amount of sand and composition. Each grain of sand has its own history and identity. Some of the sand came from the ocean or sea floor and others came from the dock you walked past moment before you gathered your sand. The way we express our sexuality will vary per person and, sometimes, the individual's interests may evolve or change. Sexuality is unique to every person.

Sexuality is meant to be explored. Sex is meant to be pleasurable. If you disagree, I am more than willing to listen to other perspectives as long as the perspective is not coming from a place of oppression or sexual dominance over others. I will argue some are fearful of talking about sex because they are not comfortable with knowing they are not pleasuring their partner properly or fear of just being wrong.

When there is little discussion about sex and pleasure, it leaves a window for misinformation to be spread. For example, discussing vaginally fingering one's partner and indicating that the person providing the fingering should jab rather than rub. And the next question for those who did not know they were doing it wrong may be, rub what? This is why proper sexual education is needed, not only for adolescence, but for adults as well.

We must learn to unravel our insecurities and shame around the topic of sex. To think we live in a world where people will happily argue against existing in a relationship where there is sexual pleasure for both parties is baffling. If anything, the argument just shows a person's insecurities and their willingness and comfort to being in a one-sided relationship. If this is you, I am sorry for the personal attack, but I will let you continue to do you. I just know, I could not do it. You are braver than me, and I respect you and the strength and patience you carry. Because, I am going to get mine.

Some may look at this statement and say I am being selfish, and I agree. This is a selfish statement, but we must be selfish sometimes. This is not saying "do not be selfless" but providing a lesson I had to learn multiple times in my life, your/my happiness, satisfaction, and pleasure matter too. Self-care is necessary.

An insecurity that many must learn to unlearn is you must give all of yourself in a relationship. If you do not take time for yourself and ensure you are pleased, you will end up becoming an empty shell of yourself until you either lose yourself in your partner, become someone you end up not liking, or burn out and your body forces you to make time for yourself. Why wait until shit hits the fan when you can make the adjustment and be selfish and recharge today. So many times, I have heard the argument that a romantic relationship is 50-50 however the same individuals are supportive in allowing the sexual relationship to be one-sided. *Where did the 50-50 go?* Just say "Communication is both ways, but I am not willing to learn how to please my partner" and stop arguing with people.

For those who feel ashamed of sex, I am here to tell you there is no need. Your curiosity on the subject is valid and you are not alone. Most people who purchased this text either (a) did so to bash it without reading it; (b) wanted to learn about sex; (c) wanted to be more sex positive; or (d) have found some offense in terms of the subject matter, but were curious about the books content. I say this to say, you are not the only one reading this book, so why feel ashamed? If anything, I believe everyone on the planet will agree at least one of the purposes for sex is to bring new life into this world. So, why is it taboo to talk about sex when that aspect of sexuality is agreed on? Yet, when the topic of pleasure pops up, there is shame and sin. And again, I am baffled.

This book is not a one-size-fits-all kind of text, but the ideas and practices discussed within these pages have helped me and many others. I would make the bold argument that one of the first steps to being more sexually positive and getting rid of the feeling of shame when discussing your pleasure is by spending time with yourself and getting to know your body. To some, this means masturbation; and, for others, it is knowing your anatomy. Take the time and explore yourself and figure yourself out. Sometimes getting to know yourself is a journey of introspection. There is no set path. Sometimes you end up doing all three depending on what stage of your life you are in. As I have mentioned previously, the way we express our sexuality varies and it may change in time.

Being sex positive does not equate to promiscuity. It can be a facet in expression, but it is not the overall purpose of being sex positive. In essence, sex positivity is just acknowledging sex as being a part of the human condition and knowing that sexuality, no matter how it is expressed, is completely normal. Additionally, sexual positivity is all about ensuring sexual encounters are both safe and consensual. Sexual positivity is removing that label that one size fits all, because it does not. Not everyone enjoys missionary position during sex. Not everyone enjoys receiving oral or giving it. Not everyone is comfortable with anal. Not everyone wants to have sex. No matter where you fall on the spectrum of how you display your sexuality, it is valid and okay.

I know there are some who may bring up their religion or spiritual practice to make an argument against being sex positive but think about why you are saying this and whether or not you are projecting. It is perfectly valid for you to feel how you feel on the issue, but your feelings are not others' feelings. They do not have to feel the way you feel. The other party is not you, which is why the very first chapter of this book is saying if it is not for you, do not try and make it for you. If you skipped the chapter, please go back and read it.

It is 100% possible to hold your religious or spiritual beliefs and be sex positive. It is 100% possible to hold your religious or spiritual beliefs and allow another person to live their life however they desire to. You do not have to support whatever *it* may be, but you must learn to accept *it* and allow others to just exist and be happy. What does it take away from any individual to be kind to another and show compassion and care? For example, if I walked out my door this morning with $300 and treated every person I made contact with like the human they are regardless of our differences, I will return home with $284 because I decided to grab a bite to eat for lunch. Other than the $16 spent on my lunch, what did I lose that day? I do not see any losses.

Another thing that may help a person figure out their sexual desires is watching porn. However, one must also understand that porn is not the most accurate portrayal of sex. Pornography is an artwork. It is a performance. It is a show. It is not a manuscript that dictates how sexual encounters unravel. I would argue that pornography is a gateway to discovering multiple sexual practices, such as BDSM (bondage and discipline, dominance and submission, sadism and masochism). Though I am not affiliated with the site, I recommend everyone take the BDSM test at least once in their life. However, it is preferable that they take it in different stages in their life because sexual interest varies.

I recommend the test because it provides explanation of your high percentage sexual pleasure archetypes and lists a percentage value in order of how likely you are to identify with such sexual practice. For example, the last time I took the test, my highest three archetypes included 100% switch, 97% brat tamer, and 96% rigger. There are other archetypes that I fell within, such as non-monogamist and dominant, but these are just a few.

Those who are unfamiliar with the test and those terms may be wondering what this means. The percentage just provides a numerical representation of how a certain archetype suits you in terms of sexual pleasure with others.

We will use my results indicating I am 100% switch. According to the BDSM test webpage, this means that I prefer to switch between being the dominant (or top position) and the submissive (or bottom position). They also say that some individuals who fall in this archetype may have a dominant play partner and a submissive play partner. A switch is a person who falls within the gray area of the spectrum between dominant and submissive. There are many other archetypes that can be learned from using the site. In a previous relationship, I used this test to see how my partner wants to be pleased, learned some tips from porn, asked them for feedback to gauge interest, and learned to make their world change every time we had sex. And the great thing about it, the sex was both pleasurable for me and them.

There is power in your pleasure. There is power in your sexuality. It is up to you to make the decision to take ownership of it. I get that we exist in a world where pleasure is taboo, but you are not the world and you deserve to live your best authentic life. Previously when I hosted conversations about sex, I would ask people to imagine they lived in a world where there are no judgments about how they choose to express their sexuality. I would pose the question, what would your life be like? Unsurprisingly, a few enthusiastically said they would be promiscuous, and others mentioned they would walk around naked. After a few people made the statement and expressed their unfiltered desire, the tension in the room increased and the judgement began. Sometimes the statement was turned into a joke and the individual laughed it off. Other times, there was an awkward silence.

Let us tackle that thing called insecurities. Over the years I have made one solid assumption about insecurities: your insecurities do not necessarily belong to you. *Now, what does that mean?* Essentially, the things that provide us with the negative energy that fuels our insecurities stem from outside forces. Our insecurities are born from how others may perceive us. For example, have you ever wanted to try something new and asked yourself, "I wonder what my friends/family might think?" and you decided not to move forward with it because you knew others would not approve? Let's call thoughts similar to these, which focuses on others' opinions, as fuel for your insecurities.

I am here to say this to the people in the back: Fuck what other people think. Live your life! I say live your life because the important term within the sentence is **your**. Those who may think negative thoughts about whatever your passions may be have their own lives to live (or ruin). Do not allow any person to have ownership of how you choose to live and express your authentic self. I hear it too often between couples where one partner is wishing to try something new to increase passion within the relationship and the other partner is focused on what their friends may think. Forget about your friends. If the friends are not a part of the sexual and romantic relationship, why does their opinion matter? The way I see it, "if you ain't trying to be in my bedroom, mind your business." If it makes you happy, go for it. If the people you are surrounded by are those who do not want you to be happy, they are the wrong people to have in your circle. Change your circle and build it based on healthy support. Whatever you need to help you break down those insecurities, find it. You deserve it. And you are wonderful.

The overall lesson here is live your life. Do not focus too much on the judgements of others, because they do not matter. Do not allow insecurities to block your happiness. Do not allow others to have the power of identifying who you are. You are you, not other's projections.

Chapter 7

Where to Start

So, the purpose of this book is to discuss how to be a hoe. This is the chapter dedicated to discussing the matter. I know, for some, they decided to skip to this chapter because it dives into the nitty-gritty. No judgement to those who skipped pages. Just make sure you go back to read the other chapters. There will be references to other sections and topics that you may need context on. But I do want all readers to sit back and relax. Listen to your favorite music. Light your favorite scented candle. Fill your room with the scent of a fresh pie from the oven. Whatever it is that puts you in a pleasant mood, do it. It is now time to start talking about how to be a hoe.

First and foremost, I need everyone to know that being a hoe is not doing reckless things from a place of hurt. Before embarking on the path of hoeing, you must first let all of your hurt go. Whatever your needed path may follow in order for you to process and deal with your hurt, take the path because the hurt has to be taken care of. I know for a fact counseling helps for hurt brought on by trauma and insecurities. Sometimes people have to let go of their hurt on a religious or spiritual level. Whatever the method, let it go.

When people tie their hurt and sexuality together, mistakes happen. Way too many times I have heard the story of a person who had a life altering sexual encounter which happened during a period of hurt. If your partner cheats on you, do not get even by doing the same. Work on yourself through whatever method that is beneficial and healthy to you.

Working on yourself includes a multitude of things. I recommend writing down a list of things you need in order to live the lifestyle of a hoe. Do you need privacy? If so, what does privacy mean to you? Does this mean a room to yourself or a home or apartment? Are there any financial concerns? If so, what are some remedies? Also, make sure you broaden your thoughts about working on yourself as much as possible. Another thing one may think about is mobility. If you are planning on expressing your sexuality with casual hook ups, are you planning on driving, being driven, or using a ride sharing service? The main idea is to have yourself in a better space, however you may define it, before you actively start hoeing.

An important question to ask yourself is why do you want to be a hoe? Are you just exploring your sexuality? Are you trying to fill a hole in your heart? Are you just trying to dog these hoes or mfs? Now, for these last two questions, I will say pause right now. If you are trying to fill a hole in your heart, it is not the right time for you. When you are trying to patch a hole in your heart with another person, it sounds like the recipe for codependency and falling for the wrong person. Sometimes our hearts lie to us and keeps us in situations that are not beneficial. Once the hole is fixed, you will then be in a better space. As for the last question, you have me messed up. Go back to Chapter 5. This is not *the game*.

The reason you should ask yourself why you want to be a hoe is to allow you the opportunity to self-reflect. This is an opportunity to truly open the internal dialogue about your intentions. And, the reason you should write out a list of things that you need to live your lifestyle as a hoe is to make sure that you have goals. Being a hoe is not something you dedicate your entire life to; however, it can be if you so choose. Most people treat their hoe-phase as a transitional phase. If you are single and making transitions towards a degree or a new home, why not enjoy your ride? Now, this does not mean you have to be promiscuous; how you express your sexuality is up to you. Regardless of who you are, hoeing or not, take time to enjoy the ride when you are transitioning to your next space.

Next up, define what being a hoe looks like for you. Does this mean having a roster (next chapter)? Does this mean multiple sex partners? Does this mean one? Does this mean strictly cuddling? Or does this mean a conversational hoe? This is the time for you to have the honest conversation about what your outcome is for going down this path. For some, this may be finding a partner who reciprocates pleasure. For others, being a hoe means finding someone to connect with on a spiritual level. Are you looking to engage in a kink or fandom? Are you planning on going on multiple dates with potential romantic partners who want to start a family business in a field you share? Are you only going to be hoeing on certain days? For example, I'm a weekend hoe. Are you just looking for someone who will happily take care of your bills?

Next up, establish rules and standards. Additionally, know your preferences, prejudices, and deal breakers. Of course, I will go into detail on each of these, but it is time to get really comfortable with yourself and build what I call the hoe door. The hoe door is essentially your door of trust.

Many of us have some form of trust issues or hesitation when it comes to blindly meeting someone, and it is understandable. The hoe door is just a simple tool to ensure no one crosses your boundaries or sets off personal red flags.

First, we will start with rules and standards. The rules are those things you are willing to allow. What is it that you need from your sexual partner(s) that will make you more comfortable around them? What is allowed within your space? What are you comfortable with tolerating? What will you not tolerate? What are your red flags? What are the consequences for violating your rules? Keep in mind, others have their own set of rules. This is why honest communication is important.

When you have figured out your rules, work on your standards. Think of standards as a condition. I say conditions because people and their personal living conditions may change on a daily basis. If the proper conditions you want a potential partner to have includes entities such as a car or job, that is perfectly fine. With conditions, you can make qualifiers. Will any job do for you? Will any car work for you? Do you want to be sure they are in comfortable living conditions? Do you want them to be independent when dating? What are the conditions the individual must meet in order for you to feel comfortable with them?

The next three terms, preferences, prejudices, and deal breakers are important to differentiate. I do not know how many times I have been on a dating app and saw racial discrimination listed as a preference. Or the amount of times I have been considered an exception because I am cute or "one of the good ones". Now, this is not to say a person is not entitled to deem what they find unattractive as unattractive, but I am here just to tell you how it is and nothing less. With that said, let's start with preferences.

A person's preferences can change over time. It may change person to person. These individuals are not exceptions, they are someone you may be attracted to. The best way to describe preferences is by thinking of different flavors of ice cream. Many of us have a favorite ice cream. Personally, I am more of a frozen yogurt person, but I love butter pecan ice cream. However, for the purposes of this example, let's say our collective favorite ice cream is chocolate. This means we prefer chocolate over other flavors; however, this does not exclude other flavors. Every once in a while, we may get a taste for vanilla or strawberry, or maybe even some butter pecan. At the end of the day, our taste is not exclusive. We just have an established preferred flavor and style.

Other times we have prejudices. Often times you see prejudices show up when there are biases or insecurities. For example, someone calls you unattractive. That is them projecting their feelings on to you. The issue here is not that you are unattractive, you are unattractive to them and that is okay. We all have our own interests. Like I mentioned in the previous chapter, do not allow anyone to take ownership of your identity. Some of the common things I have seen on social media and dating apps that show peoples prejudices include no fats, no fems, no old people, no whores, real men only, real women only, no *insert race or skin tone* people, or no ugly people. Much of this stems from personal biases, preconceived notions about a person, or social stigma.

There is an ignorance that comes with blanket statements such as these. Again, it is perfectly fine for a person to have their prejudices. If your exclusion of a certain group does not come from a personal encounter or genuine unattraction, just call your prejudice for what it is; do not try to soften it with the word preference. It is not "just a preference". Also, do your best not to stereotype people because everyone is unique. Do not block your blessings by being ignorant. I would like to add, however, if you find yourself involved with or coming across a profile with prejudices you do not support, feel free to block them. Remember what I said about keep the fish you catch on your boat? Blocking them is essentially the same thing and opens the door for a potential new fish—ones that best suit your needs.

Deal breakers are just that—a deal breaker. Do not pass go. Do not roll a second time. Do not engage. Essentially, the deal breakers are the prejudices I mentioned earlier, but there are no exceptions to the rule. Plain and simple.

The next step is the step which often surprises people. No sex. *Why would someone who has been preaching about sex and sex positivity and all that jazz suggest not having sex?* Probably because I have learned many lessons about how sex and impulsivity can become intertwined. This goes back to the first step, work on you. Know who you want and what you desire. If you need help, find a life coach, a mental health professional, someone with experience, or find trust and love within and for yourself. You set the terms on how long you wish to refrain from sex. Dedicate more time to loving yourself. If this means taking yourself out on a date, then do it. Treat yourself how you want others to treat you that way you do not make the mistake of allowing someone to hurt or damage you. This is important advice for those who are looking for love rather than sex.

The last step of being a hoe is being happy with who you are. I know a lot more people were looking for more information than what I have presented, but the way you live your life should be guided by you and only you. However, and I can't stress this enough, you should be honest and upfront about your intentions. There is no need to lead others on or waste their time. If your main focus is to find love, then find love. If you are looking to have casual sex, say so. People are often surprised at what they find when they are honest about their intentions. Regardless of your intentions, remember not to allow anyone to name you something you are not. This is them projecting their beliefs or feelings on to you and you do not have to claim it.

I do want to share a few words for those who are looking for romance and the love of their life. Always be open and honest about what you are looking for. Love does not have a set look or set conditions. Find someone who is willing to reciprocate the energy you put into them. Be sure to understand each other's likes and dislikes. Understand each other's languages. This can be textual language, body language, verbal communication style, spoken language, and cultural language. Listen to and hear each other. Show respect for each other. Love each other. Honor each other. Consent to each other. No two relationships look the same. Whatever you find within your romantic relationship that both yourself and your partner(s) enjoy, go for it. Nothing but best wishes to you all.

While I have you all here, let's talk about online dating and hoeing. Yes, there are dangers that come with online dating, which is why I recommend safe sexual encounters. You define what safety looks like for you. It can be sharing your location or using contraception. Online platforms can lead to safe sexual encounters and love. Some may find a partner by looking through their Facebook friend list, while others may use apps like Tinder. Tinder has shifted because of its users. People are no longer looking for a date and are more interested in a one-time or on-going fling. This is not to say you cannot find love on the app, just saying that it is an option. In addition to Tinder, you have POF, Badoo, some apps based off sexual orientation (for example, Grindr or Zoe), and even a cute follower from a Twitter or Instagram page. Just remember to set the terms with your potential partner. Also, if you feel the need to do so, list your intentions on your profiles. If someone does not read it, that is on them not you. In other words, live your best hoe life.

Chapter 8

Building a Roster

If you have ever heard of *the game* or being a hoe (prior to the publishing of this book), you may have heard of building a roster. Essentially, the roster is a list of people that are being played, on the field, being dogged out, or being exploited. There are very few non-toxic definitions of what a roster is outside of its culturally appropriate definition which exists in most dictionaries. My version of the roster stems from the not so culturally appropriate definitions. But, the gist of my version of the roster is honesty and informed consent.

Before going into the creation of the roster, I must touch base on how this version developed. I believe I first learned of the concept of the roster from an older cousin of mine when I was in the fourth or fifth grade. In addition to that, I was already familiar with some of the lessons involved with *the game* from overhearing conversations, recognizing trends on television shows, and being taught how to play. I guess when you add my distaste for cheating to my distaste for double standards a new way to play *the game* emerged; one based in honesty rather than literal games.

The concept of the roster I use was developed by the time I was a sophomore in high school, which was roughly in 2009. Surprisingly, it has been very beneficial. The original plan within the roster was to have a full separation between my hoe life and personal/professional life by having a separate phone. However, that can be pricy. If this is something that may help you, feel free to purchase two phones. Some prefer to do this when it comes to separating work and personal life. Whatever brings you balance and provides a comfort, do it.

When it comes to building your roster, I recommend using a method you understand. My personal choice in rosters is sports related. You may use mine if you want. Typically, when explaining the roster, I use basketball. It is a sport I enjoy watching on occasion and somewhat understand. Your roster can hold as many players as you want and may include bench warmers too. The starting lineup consists of five (5) players: point guard, shooting guard, small forward, power forward, and center. Your point guard is your go-to partner. This person is typically at the top of the list. This is the person who can satisfy you emotionally, physically, sexually, and/or mentally. Yes, I know I put physically and sexually. Not all physical contact has to be sexual intercourse.

Next up, we have the shooting guard. This is your go-to three-point shooter. This person is the back-up or number two person that serves the purpose of getting you from point A to point B. This person is the ideal friend with benefits. The last person I am going to discuss is the small forward, the other's you can look up to get an idea of making your own roster. The small forward is your most versatile player. This versatility can include actions they can perform or the fact they are most likely free at all times of the day/evening.

WARNING: I must stress that you be open and honest with those you decided to place on your roster. Do not have them thinking you are looking for a relationship when your only intent is sexual pleasure. Also, do not be afraid to bench a player or cut them from your team. Though the person is on your roster, this does not mean the individual is not a free agent. If they decide to have their own roster and you are not in support of that, discuss it with them and they have the choice to do it your way or not and you have the choice of adapting, removing yourself out of the situation, or getting over it. Again, honesty is key and so is being understanding. These are mutually agreed upon relationships. If they become one-sided, drama will likely occur.

The roster has many purposes outside of the sexual realm, as well. The individual(s) you choose to be on your roster can serve multiple purposes ranging from emotional needs to physical needs. If the roster is used properly, it is highly unlikely you'll end up getting caught up. *Why is that?* Because the basis of the roster is being open with others.

As a best practice, do not try and make your partner(s) into your therapist. When I mention emotional needs, I am mostly referring to affirmations. For example, there are people out here who only wish to see nude pictures of others with little to know desire to be in a relationship. If you need a confidence boost such as this and there is a person on your roster who fulfills this need, then do you. There is nothing wrong with this at all. Every now and then, we all need a confidence boost or something to keep us motivated on our goals. Of course, this is not to say anyone cannot make it alone. But, why be alone when you can bring your village?

Also, if you are looking to have a partner finance you, that is fine too. Just be sure everyone is clear on the terms of the relationship. For example, there are plenty of people willing to pay money for photos of feet. This is not shaming those people. I support all of it. If your first thought was, that is not a bad idea and you shame sex workers, then make sure you have read Chapter 3. There should be no shame in how a person willingly expresses their sexuality. If someone is willing to pay me $100 million for a video of me clapping two ass cheeks and flipping a titty, I am going to take it. If you see the video, mind your business.

Remember, when deciding if you are going to create a roster, define your comfort zone. How intimate are you looking to be with those on your list? What are you looking for? Are you sure that this is the thing for you? These are important questions that you would need to answer before committing to having a list. Before you are able to tell your partner(s) what your intentions are, you have to know them yourself. Before you can set the expectation of your partner(s) to be upfront and honest, you MUST be honest with yourself. If you are a person looking to find "the one", the roster is of no help to you.

Now, the honesty you are looking to have with your partner(s) is full disclosure on where things are going between the two of you. Do you have to let them know how many others are on your roster? Not necessarily. But, if both of you are comfortable with disclosing this information then why not? Keep in mind you must set your ground rules. Let them know that you are not looking for anything serious. Having a roster is not one of those but-you-never-know-what-may-happen things. This is where people tend to get themselves caught up. By making statements like this, you leave the door open for the possibility of a relationship. This is not to say that it is not possible that one may catch feelings for the other. If one of those but-you-never-know-what-may-happen things do happen, then it is time to evaluate your next steps. Are you planning on being exclusive? Is it time to exit the hoe phase? Are the feelings mutual? It is possible this may occur so do keep this in mind. By establishing your intention upfront, this ensures that all parties are on the same page. Along with this, NEVER make it seem as though they are the only one you are involved with, be it sexual, emotional, or just social. This does not mean that it is implied, this means you should inform them.

With having a roster, catching feelings for one or more of your partner(s) is a possibility. Sadly, you cannot fight physiology. *What does physiology have to do with anything?* Physiology has everything to do with human nature and catching feelings for another person. The more you are around someone, the more likely for your hormones to begin to activate and possibly make associations.

I am going to take this moment to be scientifically informal. So, there is this hormone called oxytocin, also known as the "cuddle hormone". LET ME TELL YOU ABOUT THIS SHIT. This hormone does a lot of things, ranging from assisting in child labor to child rearing. Oxytocin, according to a study I read, may play a role in preventing infidelity. Oxytocin is released when one is cuddling, or even through social bonding. It is even released when you are playing with a dog. So, obviously, get yourself a dog if you are not trying to "catch feelings" for one of your partners. I am just kidding. Let's bring it on back to reality now. For more information, I do recommend doing further research on oxytocin. It really is not as scary as I am presenting it. Oxytocin is a pleasure hormone, if anything. And pleasure has many different forms, cuddling is just one.

The cuddle hormone is not your enemy. In fact, it has benefits to your health in terms of reducing stress. Again, the more you are around your partner(s) the more likely feelings will emerge; either for yourself or them. There is no way to prevent this. My only recommendation is to see the person less but not to exclude them. You can possibly revamp their role on the roster or within your life. If you are ever in the predicament where you wish to go "all in", or start a relationship, with one of your partners or your partner, discuss this with the individual beforehand. If they wish to continue, inform the others on your list, if any, that your interactions with them are over. This will help you prevent any misunderstandings and keep you from getting caught up when there is absolutely nothing to be caught on. Some former relationships develop into platonic friendships and others may gradually fade out.

This tip is random but needed. If you choose to have a roster, do not use pet names like sweetie, babe, boo, honey, or bae. Know their names and use them. If you have already had the discussion that they are not the only one you are seeing, they will already understand if you have a slight hiccup and use the wrong name. It is less likely to happen when you associate a person with their actual name rather than a pet name. It will also help if you do the same for their names in your phone. Instead of using some kind of secret code using words of association or emoji's, get a contact picture from them; that way, every time they message or call, you can associate the name with the face. But this advice is not useful for those who wish to cheat. If that is you, sorry, this advice is not for you.

Chapter 9

The Benediction of Hoeing

As I sit here, writing—enjoying a bowl of soup and sipping on some blue Powerade—I am shocked I am ending my book sooner than I expected. The topic of sexuality and its expression has ridden my anxiety for damn near all my life and I can only dedicate less than 50,000 words in arguing a case for hoeing and positive sexuality. Well, I am actually just making a case for the importance of consent, identifying sexual violence, and eradication of negative sex work practices. Rather than writing on ways to find a work life balance that is inclusive of sex, which I recommend for you all to look into, I am taken aback by the purpose of me writing this book.

The purpose of me writing this book is to open a dialogue and educate. I have always been, in some fashion or the other, an educator. Specifically, I am writing this book for a target audience: Black, masculine presenting, people who subscribe to toxic masculinity. Now, me making this statement is not saying I am against Black men or men of any race. I am just putting my focus on my community because there's much we need to work on fixing for ourselves that others are not trying or willing to help us with.

Let it be known this text has been written by a Black bisexual cisgender man, and I love my community dearly. I know what I discussed in this book in terms of toxic behaviors is not culturally or racially specific, but I refuse to center whiteness. I doubt I even have the energy to do so. Anyone who finds the previous statement problematic, then that is your drama and do not project it on me.

This text has been written to engage others regardless of where they come from because we all have some toxic traits to unlearn in some way—myself included. Trust and believe that I thought about how this book will be looked at way before sitting down to write it. Granted, some time has passed but I see the same issues rather than growth. It is time for things that are done in the dark to come to light. When we shine a light on the issues and fight to make positive changes, we all see growth. But, as we are now, the systemic issues are standing tall. Before I continue in this benediction, I want to say thank you to all who have chosen to read this book or purchased it out of hate. I appreciate you. Feel free to stop reading at this point because I came here to shake some muthafucking tables. Luckily, I built my own, so I am good.

When I think on the history of this country and the many times a voice has been silenced, I am amazed. I am grateful for the resilience and the power that comes within my ancestry. I type these words unafraid because I have no time for fear these days. No matter how many people try and silence my voice, I know it will continue to yell in those who are inspired. I can die tomorrow and still have peace of mind because I know there is not a person alive that can calm my power. The same power that exists in many marginalized people, especially, Black people.

In reading this book, you saw some of the issues that need to be fixed within the United States. I just want to name other issues that need to be fixed as well. First off, let's bring up the criminal justice system. How many studies need to be done before we fix the system? Or does the system enjoy toying with the lives of the poor and broken people (there's a difference). Numbers of people are put into the prison system who are innocent or doing a ridiculous amount of time behind bars just for existing, having marijuana, or being in the wrong place at the right time for convenience and blame. But we say this system is fair and continue to ignore the research. Torturing people is a choice not a requirement.

It is baffling that we cannot create a system of justice where a person can do time, seek mental health counseling, continue their education, encourage positive human interactions which assists in joining the workforce, and allow people who made a mistake to learn and still enjoy the beauty of life. I know there are programs that are making these transitions, but this needs to be a standard. I am tired of the PR stunts. My blackness and existence are not a talking point for political games. Additionally, Black lives matter is a factual statement not a talking point for gaslighting and firing up a base. I will refrain from going further into politics because it is not my strong suit. But I am ready to see these reparations that have yet to come through policy, economic wealth, education, health care…you know what, let me just stop here and return to my benediction. If you are looking for wonderful political commentary shows, I recommend Burn it Down with Kim Brown, Clickbaity Political Thirst Trap, and the Young Turks.

In wrapping up this book, I want you all to continue your introspection. Allow yourself time to rationally think and exist. Sometimes you just have to focus on where you are now before you can plan out where you will be tomorrow. Remember the very first question you must ask yourself prior to embarking on the path: why do you want to hoe? How are you going to get to your desired space prior to hoeing? What does your hoeing look like? What are the conditions you require? What is on your list? What are your intentions for hoeing? And my last question for you, are you happy and satisfied?

For those who have read up to this point, again I must say thank you. The purpose of Slaytor Jackston is providing an opportunity for untold stories. Slaytor Jackston is a way of allowing those who have been silenced the opportunity to scream. Though this book is the first published by Slaytor's Playhouse, LLC, it will not be the last. For those who wish to tell their story detailing their lived experience up to their liberation from unjust human trafficking, I invite you to reach out to Slaytor's Playhouse. If you are a sex worker willing to highlight your positive and negative experiences, I invite you to reach out. If you are a writer of erotica and want your book published by Slaytor's Playhouse, I invite you as well. If you are a researcher in sexuality and wish to submit your research, I invite you to do so (be mindful the research will be available to the public for free).

This book is only the start. There are other projects in the works, and I am excited to share them with you all when the time comes. I recommend following Slaytor's Playhouse on Instagram at SlaytorsPlayhouse or follow Slaytor Jackston on twitter at JacktheSlay.

Please leave your reviews of the book. Give me your worst but also give me your best. I am sending love to all and best wishes. If your table has been shooketh, let us all hope, it is not taken from you.

About the Author

I am not the typical author. In an ordinary book, the "About the Author" section tends to tell you about the authors credentials, previous work, and their history. But that is not the type of author that I am. I am sure many of you have realized this by now. I am weird and I love that about myself. Rather than telling you who I am, I would rather show you. This section will contain a collection of poems I have written throughout my life leading up to January 23rd, 2021 and will be found in the print version of the book. If you have purchased the eBook, the title of the collection is "Prose from a Soul Seeking Justice" and is available as an eBook. Not every poem has been workshopped, some are even unedited. I chose to do this because we become different people at every stage of our lives. I am just happy I was able to read each poem and reflect. I was able to see my growth and appreciate it. As I have said before, I appreciate you for purchasing this book. I hope you have learned a lot and hope you are able to understand my truth. I look forward to the many publications that will come in the future from Slaytor's Playhouse, LLC.

With that being said, who is Vernon T. Scott?

Prose from a Soul Seeking Justice

Vernon T. Scott

SLAYTOR'S
PLAYHOUSE

Prose from a Soul Seeking Justice

Sorrowful Sunday
(unedited)

Sunday:
You ventured to the hospice near Doctors Hospital
We were sad because you weren't doing so well
I cried as I watched as your chest rose and fell
You said you didn't want to see us cry so I went outside
There were others who also cried yet we were spiritually by your side
After hours of crying we began reminiscing about the past
Not know which minute will be your last

Monday:
After school, We visited you once more
To see you awake filled my heart with joy
Until dark we listening to music and watching shows of your choice
Yet we would have been talking if you had your voice

Tuesday:
Once again I visited you at the hospice
Still happy to see you as if being overwhelmed twice
Your mother was there your sisters too...
We enjoyed our time without a slight boo-hoo

Wednesday:
We venture to see you in your room
Yet we had to wait because there was too many people visiting you
We waited awhile for people to leave
I was so happy and so very relieved
We only talked for only a moment
Yet that moment was a time well spent

Thursday:
Today when we visit people from the church were there
So I stayed in the room to pray for your care

Friday:
To day at school I was talking with a friend
I told her I will rather go before you met your end
We visited with news that you were sleeping
Before we left I watched you sleep instead of weeping

Saturday:
I was at my aunts house
We visited at an early hour but the nurse had change your blouse
After she finished we said our hellos
Then we left for the day not knowing what will follow

Sunday:
We were playing a game on the Nintendo
Until we received a call that brought about my sorrow
It appears that you had past away on May 6, 2007 near the hour of 11
But I was so very said even though I knew you were on your way to heaven
I ventured home eyes red and all
I went past the computer room that's when the tears began to flow
Though no one at school really knew about what happen except for a few
But when they found out, they said it was brave for me to come to school knowing all that I was going through
Yet they didn't know at all the way I really felt

Middle and High School

For each night I cried to to ease my way through the pain that was dealt
I cried each night until the funeral on the following Saturday
I cried all my tears of sadness on those day before
So on your home coming celebration I could cry tears of true joy
Though I'm still sad that you are no longer with me
I'm happy that I'll see you once again
So to my dear Mother, P███████████████, I wish for you always to rest in peace

Respect

Why should I care about the things you say?
I liked it much better when I didn't see you everyday
We both have our own separate lives
So, you live your and I'll live mine

Respect works two ways, inwards and out
If you cared for me, then I wouldn't have to shout
You never listen to anything that I say
I could tell you I've been shot, and sarcastically you'll say okay

If there is no trust within the family where can you find it
It's not that I'm a liar, it's because you're full of shit
You can't tell when I'm sad, mad, or angry
So how can you tell when you don't know me?

Day in and day out all you do is bitch
Yet, you have the nerve to get mad when I catch a fit
You never see the things that you do
So, what kind of father figure are you?

You tell my brother and I not to talk back
Yet, I see you do that to your mother, yet she shows you respect
You are one lazy man
You work three days a week and complain

You think you hold all types of power
But the only thing you hold is bitter and sour
You cuss for no reason
From season to season

You need to get a life and stop being so mean
Yet, appearances can be tricked, but some true colors are always seen
I started this poem without a way to end
Well, I have one word, and it's "FIN"

Sorrow for you

Life is what God gives and takes away
For life is completely hard to live day by day
But why is it hard? Can it be easy? Is there such a way?

Life is full of evils with not so many angels to help ease your way
But so many angels are being born but that means some fade away
Yet, evil is spread from those who let anger lead their way

Another soul turned toward darkness and no longer sees day
Yet we try to remind them of our love and we pray
But can we help that dark soul who has lost their way?

Passage of Time

You start at the beginning and skip the middle
in order to see the end.
Your mind is set on your past and your future
never the present which bends.
The present holds all your ambitions and dreams,
Yet, you look pass that for what you can redeem.

You look to the past for memories but not guidance;
overlooking what is now will not bring you to an alliance.
The thing you wanted you cannot yet achieve.
It's because skipping around won't put you in the lead.

You live for tomorrow
but it might just bring more sorrow.
Learn to live for today
where there is still time to play.

Deep Secrets
(unedited)

Ugh people always tell you secrets that should never be told
From being from the past or something that's not so old
But those thing we know as being a deep secret
Is not a deep secret at all
When the person slips up and tell what they heard you call them a traitor
But what is the point I ask are you not the hater
The secret you told
Be it sad or bold
Is not your deepest secret
For your deepest secret is your soul

Freedom

Why must you lie to me?
Why won't you quit and set yourself free?
You say it is nothing. It helps for relieving stress and it's a time well spent.
Yet, I tell you that this is not true. You should make a better commitment.
You lie to yourself by saying you're not committed;
For the activities you do are better and it fits to your schedule.
I tell you that it is your desire and the bringer of your despair,
But all you do is shut me up and try not to speak of this affair.
You blame the world for the pain that was afflicted,
Yet, you cannot see that you're addicted.
You are committed to drugs but not to life
And can't realize that is what caused your pain and strife.
You said quitting once was your desire.
So, how come you're still lighting the fire?
I hoped for better days for you;
But, I understood that it was something only you can do.
I waited and waited for your commitment to release
But now I stare down at this grave for the decease.
I have something to tell you my dear friend, "REST IN PEACE".

The Makings of a Gentleman

What does it mean to be a gentlemen? A person who respects his woman and those around him? A gentleman is someone who is responsible and able to be relied upon. Many men call themselves a gentleman, yet they forget that the word is composed of two separate words that both have different meaning.

Gentle, being the first word, means having a kind character. Gentle is having the courage to show emotion. A person that is gentle is also quite calm.

What is a man? A man is a person that is strong yet weak. A man is flexible. He is the proverbial tree caught in a hurricane. Strong winds will make it bend, but once the storm is over it stands tall.

What is a gentleman? You have the answer. A gentleman is able to bend and stand tall once they're needed. A person who can show his true emotions. So, are you a gentleman?

Torn Between 2 Rights With No Wrong
(unedited)

How am I suppose to love justice and not love trust
Not loving trust will bring the unjust
But not loving Justice will bring deviousness
So how should I know which one is best

Can I chose between these 2
As if I had 1 clue
I'll love to choose the one that supplies hope above all things
But who can tell me that one will bring peace with wings

How can I choose which one will bring joy
Choosing the right one is not like choose a simple toy
Why should I bother with this helpless choice
Yet I still refuse to listen to the third voice

It says why choose what can not be sure
But make a decision that is easier than opening a door
You have another choice...the choice of three
I chose the third chose, I chose ME

The Other Level

A sparkle of interest, the seed of a tree
That blossomed in happiness and joy.
My love for you is unconditional
And by your side, is where I wish to be.
When my eyes landed on you I never thought much, yet
When I heard your voice, such emotion was felt.
Was it anger, lust for pleasure, or conquest I sought?
Or, was it the sweet melody of love
That brought me to worship at your feet?
My longing for love at last will stop
With an answer of yes. I will throw you my rope;
Tie it to your finger, forever fixed we shall be
As our blossoming tree grows exponentially.

Faith or Sin

The tide brings us in
with an unforgiving wave;
producing problems.

Sins wash away with
a neutrality known as
one's unfaithfulness.

Build a new bridge that
will force us to recognize
our unlawful path.

Suffering

I am the one who must suffer.
I feel the knife in your spleen
though it is not my flesh that
is being pierced. It hurts. I feel fire
around the open wound. Do you
feel the pain; cause I do. Do you
feel mine? Do you sense the lonely
soul? I feel yours, and it is strong.
Hide your pain like the squirrel who
waits for winter to approach. Even
though it is hidden, that does not mean
it will be forgotten. It's still there,
and I sense it. I guess I will suffer.

Philadelphia

It was an industry with a
beautiful sun roof. Though
it's reputation was bad, its
winters were memorable. I long
for its soft, slush of snow.

Pantoum
(unedited)

It bothers me that you could not stay
with me. My life has been decided years
before I came into being. These days
when I long for you to bear

with me. My life has been decided. Years
flying on the eagle's wings, sure to arrive
when I long for you. To bear
such pain is not the way I wish to live;

flying on the eagle's wings. Sure to arrive
in an unconventional manner - our style.
Such pain is not the way. I wish to live.
You take away that choice while

in an unconventional manner. Our style
before I came into being. These days
you take away that choice, while,
it bothers me that You could not stay?

Cracked
(unedited)

It's an eggshell. Strong. Durable.
With enough pressure it cracks.
The remnants of what was
has become an empty foreshadowing
of how it will forever remain.
Our conversations are now empty,
unknown by you, strongly seen
by myself, wielder of the observant
eyes, ears – eggshell. Yes, I am your
shell. I kept you stable, and
attempted to keep you from splashing
on a hard surface; wounded.

I was only your buffer.
But it ended. I no longer wanted to
be your shell. What was
platonic is no more. I am the trash;
the least important. With me is where
our friendship lie, in the trash –
discarded eggshell.

Mistaken Stranger

This breeze flows north,
but it is not the North Winds.
It has power, and color.
It whistles with wild, willowy songs –
songs that sing sweet sorrow
to the lives of the forgiving. It is
blue, yet not unhappy. It is red
and lacks aggression, anger,
and angst. It is yellow but bares
no smile. This breeze is an
invader. Secrets flow. It confides. It caresses
the skin - not in love, pleasure, or lust -
but as a means of connecting.
It hugs you like a mother. Warm.
Smooth. Loving. This breeze flows north,
but is not the North Winds.

Challenge Accepted
(unedited)

Tonight, I challenged God.
I told him if I woke up
the next morning I must have a purpose
on this Earth. I medicated.
Two ibuprofens, a shot of NyQuil,
and some sips of vodka.
I knew these things were not going to kill
me. I knew I would survive.
My challenge was not for me to die, but for me
to be renewed. I wanted to wake in pain, agony,
my guts pulling themselves out of my throat.
I wanted the experience of having my stomach
pumped. I wanted to feel something.

I cried last night. I wanted to be the person remembered.
I wanted to be eulogized, mourned, victimized.
My life had no meaning other than to help
those who wished to spit in my face. I had earned
the role of the oppressor,
though I would never do such a thing.

I am the oppressed, but my identity
is forever taken by my oppressor. He gives me
his title. My oppressor never does anything wrong.
It is always my fault. Yet, I cried last night.

My oppressor hammered the numbers 12-13 into my back.
The year of my ultimate downfall.
My oppressor – sorry, I used the wrong title –
the oppressed was the bringer. The oppressed
verbalized his hatred. He gave me a new name.

Prose from a Soul Seeking Justice

He named me fat, nigger, faggot, dike, coon, and bitch.
But it was okay for him to do so, he was
the oppressed. What good would it do for me
to have an identity? I am the oppressor.
I kept the walkways and living areas free
of litter, but the oppressed was not happy;
the whip fell to my back. I insured that the oppressed
was kept safe, but I was left out in the cold.
I sent encouragement, though I was spat
on and kicked in the ribs. I listened
to the oppressed's troubles, but the abuse
was soon to emerge again. The abuse always
varied between verbal and emotional trauma.

I thought of the knife again, last night.
It was during the crying festival
that I became accustomed to.
This time, the knife went vertical.
The knife never touched my skin,
but mentally, the knife ran through
my skin plenty of times.
More like eighty-five or more times.
The knife was an old friend of mine.
He was named the liberator. His task
was to set free the oppressed from his
oppressor, which was me. The only way
to do that was to kill the oppressor.

Suicide was no solution to this problem.
Those who commit suicide were said
to be heading to hell. Why would I want
to go back into the situation I was already in?
12-13 was my hell. I was whipped for not
being too clean. Spat on for holding back

College

harsh words. Kicked for caring too much.
Shot for being too much of a friend.
Stabbed for lying to myself
about the oppressed's comings
and goings. Stripped of my humanity
for trying to see the oppressed in a better light.

Last night, I challenged God.
When I woke up, I felt disappointed.
I wanted to feel something again.
But, what I felt was all the pain that I
became accustomed to thanks
to the oppressed; my oppressor.

Tempest
(unedited)

The breeze moves us forward.
It is my body that does the movement.
No, it is the wind and the clouds.

The hollow core of the funnel spews
garbage like a drunkard. A house,
a home, car, no, a plane flies by. What is this?

It is a gray coloration brought on by the clouds
above. It is a bear, a tree, a dog, a family?

No, it is a tempest.

Suffocation

The bee is trapped
in the barrel at
the bottom of the
lake; the barren
abyss of nothingness.

It prepares for the blast
of explosive lifelessness. But water
continues to seep in. Its fate is in cubic
feet – slowly depleting. Obscene is
the bee's life. Depravity and death awaits us.

First Entry
(unedited)

Her eyes brown, with a glow
of orange; almost as if she
was plotting something sinister.

Her skin soft. A kind
of silk I wanted to rub across my skin
in an almost repetitive motion.

Her touch moist, warm, and endless.
Something every man
wished was wrapped around him.

Her movements slow.
They began to increase as more experience
was gained by feeling more comfortable and free.

Her eyes a hazel color better seen now that the shade has fallen.
Her skin soft with a small portion of roughness that needs to be hit.
Her touch caresses my body as hers mimics my actions and convulses.

Her movements stalled.
She catches her breath.
Memories of last night.

Burn

The fire died.
Remnants of the past
died with it.

Do I miss the images?
The anger you caused?
The pain that you dealt?

Am I sorry for flames?
Sorry for the gasoline?
Sorry for the match?

Did the fire die
because of me?
Why should it?

I started the fire and it died.
Remnants of the past died with it.

Breaking In

She said no, no, no. What was heard was yes.
Blood slowly drained from the cavern
as the last sign of innocence
fades into darkness. She was trapped under the weight
of a tree trunk, almost breathless.
The trespasser's voice scraped its sound
into the crevices of her brain.

She said no, no, no. What was heard was yes.
The trespasser placed his genitalia in her face,
a face that once shined with a light.
This light was weakening. She
looked like a worn-down possum. She was different.
A woman? He slapped her in the face,
and she squirmed to be set free out of disgust and fear.

She said no, no, no. What was heard was yes.
Her wrists burned from being forced
down; trapped on her back.
She lies there, her breath deep with sobs.
Her arms were motionless strings
that were not able to fight back.
She prayed for death to come smoothly.

She said no, no, no. What was heard was yes.

Be Still

She was blue.
Breath was the thing that we wanted but it never showed.
The chest cavity was fully developed
without ever having the chance to function like
those that surrounded her (Breathe). The line of consciousness
and unconsciousness was blurred due to the lack of never having lived
on this planet, but the line motioned towards the unfavorable outcome
that we all knew was present in her body (Breathe).
A cold stone emerged from a place of warmth
and life (Still).

Hi, My Name is Jack
(unedited)

As my pen sat on the paper,
I began to think about my first victim.
I wondered about how it felt
when my knife sliced her throat.
I remembered the crimson river
that sparkled with diamonds.
This river was the most beautiful river
that I'd ever set my eyes on.

I thought about the pain
she was experiencing. It seemed
as though she was in bliss.
The knife went through her as if her neck
was a pillow; a smooth sheet. This beautiful bejeweled,
  crimson river
flowed with ease. It was as though it wanted
me to set it free. But the pain behind it...

In a way, pain decreased as it
moved towards the head. A stumped toe
felt like a planetary collision.
Yet, a bullet to the back of the head
was said to be painless.
A knife to the throat should feel like a feather.
It should tickle her soul. Maybe, the bejeweled,
crimson river rushed out because of the sweet
touch of a feather.

I remembered her moans of pleasure.
I was not aroused by them. This was her
job. She was the filth of the streets;

College

a predestined harlot. The number of men
that witnessed her body was immense. She was a woman
who never had innocence. She lost her virtue
in the arms of her mother; in the sheets of her fathers.
My beautiful bejeweled, crimson river
wanted me to deliver it from its diseased body.

Her screams when she saw the knife
approach her aroused me; filled me with joy.
Her screams were a beautiful melody.
Her first scream was the soprano note
on durme, her last scream was the alto
note of sin ansia y dolor.

With her last scream replaying in my mind,
the bejeweled, crimson river flowing, I penetrated
her body once more. I enjoyed it.
Her river stopped flowing. I wanted more of it.
I opened her chest and abdomen and searched throughout
  her body
looking for more. I found her stomach. I found
improperly chewed foods. It was as if she only swallowed
her food whole. I needed to see my river again.

I finally found it when I pulled out her heart.
I squeezed it in my palms. It was a beautiful sight.
I sewn her body closed, knowing I will not find
more of the bejeweled, crimson river within her.
I searched for it in every body I preyed
upon after her. I guessed that the bejeweled,
crimson river was only present in a virgin kill.
I turned to my paper and began to write.

Hi, my name is Jack...

Just Another
(unedited)

It's the fierce pound of the trigger,
as his lifeless body lies on the side of the road.
Hey look, it's just another nigger.

His brain is on the pavement, go figure.
He tried his best to listen to what was told
by his mother. But, too late. The trigger

was pulled, ending a life that was more than meager.
People watched him as his mother took hold
of his lifeless body. But hey, it's just another nigger.

Who knows whether he would have been a leader?
Or had a family and lived to be ninety years old?
Then again, he didn't pull the trigger.

The violence of the streets is only growing bigger
with each gang formed; with guns repping how bold
they are. But hey, it's just another nigger.

What is he now, other than another chalked up figure
drawn on the side of the road?
He had no gun, he pulled no trigger.
It's okay, he's just another nigger.

Rebirth

The sun brings forth new lives
into a young world. This world becomes diseased,
leaving its inhabitants suffering.
The sun sends out its heat
in the form of a breath
to heal us from the ice.

Beaming down on those crystallized in ice
hoping for a new life to live,
the sun becomes a whisper and breathes
shallowly. The disease
takes its course. We watch the homeless man as he eats
in an alley. The sun is failing. We mock his suffering.

He's too poor to know what it means to suffer.
Hearts become ice —
the sun still failing. We run to our homes, our heaters.
The man no longer lives
the way he did before He diseased
him and force the man to exist in disheartened breaths.

Worship the sun, the Son, the breathing
breeze. The man stopped the way he suffered.
It changed. It's a newer disease
that is thrice as big as the sun's eyes.
The wind whisks as if on a live
feed produced on a hot day displaying heat

waves on the pavement. Is it a manageable heat?
The sun thrives, but the Poor cannot breathe.
It was a beautiful day for those who lived their lives
on the inside. The poor homeless man still suffers.

The false beauty of what you or I see
is the truth behind the man's disease.

The prognosis is not fair in the diseased
man. The sun and the man become heated;
our hearts still iced like a Starbucks' coffee.
Shallow, staggering, dry, heaving, burn. Breathe.
His lungs collapsing. Ode to Suffering Poor.
The sun, with its lack of humanity, ignores the lost lives.

The man, lives no more.
Civilization continues ignoring his suffering;
his cries of help through breathlessness.
We, in ourselves, are the diseased.
We leave others to be held in heat
and trapped in agony. We look down on those frozen in ice.

Standing Empire

My inner being is a hunter...
It captures your glance
It captures your soul
It captures your smile

My inner being is a gatherer...
It keeps your secrets
It keeps your love
It keeps your dreams

My inner being is a warrior...
It fights for your needs
It fights for your happiness
It fights for your safety

My inner being is a peasant...
It is the building block that makes up a nation
It is the foundation of the ideal lover
It is the beauty that is most coveted

My inner being is a...
I want to say emperor, but I thought that was you
But there can only be one emperor
Sorry, but you do not fit the position

My inner being conquers over my insecurities
It strengthens my self worth
It builds my character
If my inner being does all of this, what is the purpose of having you?

My Blackness

Let me tell you about my blackness
It's strong
It's powerful
It's beautiful
It continues to flourish into greatness
My blackness is birthed and raised and cannot be imitated
My blackness is unconquerable
My blackness is royalty; it's just and proud
My blackness is character, not coon, mammy, or hound
My blackness is not categorized
My blackness cannot be held back and will embrace life and be free
Unless you haven't realized, my blackness is me

SKIN
(unfinished but done)

What exactly are you afraid of?
Is it the fullness of my lips?
The greatness in my eyes?
Is it the kinks in the hair?
The cornbread in the thighs?
I guess it must not be any of those.

But honestly, what are you afraid of!?
Is it the way I stay strong?
The way I'm unbothered by hate?

Being Black right now

Being Black right now:
Is being in high states of anxiety during the Christmas season and hoping and praying we will all come together and sing fah-who-doe-ray but realistically knowing that shit won't happen.

Being Black right now:
Is waking up every fucking day with universes of rage weighing on you while persevering through life; doing your best to live happy and uninterrupted but often reminded that your very existence is called radical.

Being Black right now:
Is seeing how the courts were able to see all of these ridiculous election fraud cases but do not have the time {let me gather myself} the time to see cases about false imprisonments outside of the one "charitable" PR release around the holidays to create a false sense of security and joy.

Being Black right now:
Is realizing how the external hate received over the years created a self-hatred so strong it forged a figure only to be known as imposter which resulted in self-isolation; meanwhile, the cure to this syndrome was having a safe space that FINALLY allowed you to have healthy engagements with your community; however, there's a fiery passion of hurt which continues to exist from knowing this community was strategically targeted and forced into hating itself.

Being Black right now:

Is knowing or being that kid who sold candy to all the other kids to either learn financial literacy from their parent or learn the art of hustle to survive {let's call them Tyrone} Yet, Tyrone was placed in detention, suspended, or expelled and taken from their education; meanwhile, all the other kids are encouraged to go door to door to ask for "charitable" donations for an overpriced candy bar which paid for an overpriced gadget that is cheaper than the work put in {sigh} just to be compared to the other kids and/or be unseen.

Being Black right now:
Is reading countless articles about the Black experience written by people gaining notoriety off the suffering of your people; yet, already being aware of the Black experience and knowing there's no need to prove the Black experience because all people really have to do is shut up and listen.

Being Black right now:
Is having your multiple lived experiences exploited and made into talking points. Black Lives Matter may be a movement, but it is also a fact so do NOT forget that.

Being Black right now:
Is being raped, assaulted, imprisoned, and murdered based off the fears of weak minded people who must perform a type of mental gymnastics in order to justify your death when the only thing you are guilty of is having the audacity to exist and live your best, beautiful Black life.

Being Black right now:
Is sending I love you texts to your family hoping they respond because muthafuckers are out here dying from a disease and a seditious, supremacist mentality; yet, also

making sure your family knows you love them just in case mutherfuckers decide to jump stupid or you fall ill.

Being Black right now:
Is being told regularly that we are living in our last days and refusing to accept that perspective because you desire to live your beautifully-abundant Black life.

Being Black right now is being strong regardless of the circumstances because we will overcome.

Who am I?
(unedited)

I am the parent that never procreated.
I am the activist who makes change without being activated.
I am the sibling to many though our parents are not the same.
I am the child of many, even though I am not of their seed nor egg.
I am the abused and the hurt.
I am the hatred and fake.
I am a child of God.
I am the beaten and unheard.
I am the pain and tears.
I am the sorrow.
I am the universe that surrounds me.
I am a creation in solid form that is constantly vibrating because my atoms do not stop.
I am the cradler of hatred who knows it as my kin because it is born when love meets anger; unfortunately for some, love was divorced and anger married fear.
I am the shroud of self-degradation that resulted in actions and behaviors untrue to who I am.
I am those who are forgotten and twisted into an image that is a misrepresentation of their character.
I am…I do not know anymore.

Who am I but another person who had to forget their greatness in order to dim themselves in order to survive in a sea of mediocrity?

Who am I but a healed wound that continues to bleed because my trauma is generational, and the more I heal a new trauma forms; will I ever stop bleeding?

Who am I but a person rediscovering themselves and loving the character that is forming?

Who am I? This is a question only I can answer. Regardless of the degree or authority any other individual may hold, they do not have the power to answer.

Justice, who am I?

A song for Mama
(unedited)

I want to think of this poem as an extension of Sorrowful
  Sunday.
But, in actuality, it is not.
The sorrow of that poem still holds my pain and my hurt.
The poem holds my truth and remains unedited.
I would love to change it and fix some of its imperfections,
however, in doing so I will be editing my pain which feeds
  my passions.

I was told that I should write you a letter,
but I could never sit down and write it.
I was scared and I was weak.
But then I had a revelation.
The language between you and I existed through television,
  music, and food.
The language between you and I is poetic; it is poetry.

The first song I wish to share is the one I sang so high.
Sometimes I feel like a motherless child.
I am a long way from home because you were that home.
Which leads us to the next song which is by my favorite
  male artist Luther Vandross.
I lived in many houses and none of them were that home
  that I needed.
I know now that part of it was because you were not there,
However, the rest of it was due to my failure to show up for
  myself.

I hated you for leaving, even though it was not your choice.
At times, I thought it was.

Not because you hated living, but because you were just simply tired.

But at the same time, I still hated you for leaving.

I hated you because I was the motherless child that stayed quiet

in order to keep things from becoming awkward.

I hated you because I forced myself to be silent.

I hated you for not teaching others how to love me as you did.

Which bring up another musician, Musiq Soulchild.

I screamed and sang to the top of my lungs, "teach me how to love".

Teach me how to survive in this world.

Teach me how to move on.

Teach me how to love myself.

Teach me how to forgive and forget in order to continue to grow.

Teach me how to forgive a man who said I did not love you,

solely because I made the decision to smile at your funeral rather than cry.

Teach me how to forgive those who sat idly by and did nothing to heal my depression.

Teach me how to forgive myself for wanting to die.

Teach me how to forgive the culture of ignorance.

Teach me how to love.

Thankfully, I learned. Unfortunately, it was hard.

Queue Lyfe Jennings.

The man who was able to help me survive and learn the lessons you were unable to teach me.

Up Until Now

The last song we ever sang together was "Must be nice".
I am appreciative of this memory.
This memory allowed me to find the light to love again,
and love you regardless of your shortcomings and short life.

It is crazy to think I avoided hearing this song for most of high school.
I did not want to cry. But life is crazy.
The more I avoided the song, the more Lyfe's songs kept appearing.
I think the greatest gift from Lyfe Jennings was the reminder it is okay to cry.

Therefore I did.
I let the tears run down.

I cried knowing the last movie we saw together was Dream Girls.
I cried knowing that our last meal together was leftovers.
I cried knowing that I could never come out to you.
I cried knowing that you could not see me enter high school.
I cried knowing you did not get to see me go to my 8th grade prom.
I cried because you never got to meet any of my best friends.

But, I stopped crying when I remember the last words you told me.
You told me not to cry.
I remembered the conversation you had with me when you told me to start smiling more.
I remembered how people would tell me I have your smile.
In some way, you reminded me to be happy.

So here we are. A song for mama.
A song that is telling your mother how much you love her.
So, here I am. Mama, you know I love you.

I love you for raising me to never forget my blackness.
I love you for wanting me to be educated.
I love you for your flaws and your courage.
I love you for your support and care.
I love you for refusing to allow injustice.

I love you for losing both your job in healthcare and your licensure because you stood up for an elderly patient who was being abused by a white medical professional at the clinic you worked at. But they refused to believe you or the patient.
I love you for remaking yourself and learning a new trade.
I love you for being a small business owner.
I love you for standing up and showing love to every person who came into your orbit.
I love you for moving us around. From the trailer park to a house, you maintained a sense of home.
I love you for creating a step team just for me; allowing me to do more activities that made me happy.
I love you for the one time you asked me to drop off that one erotica book to your friend who was subbing at my middle school.
I love you for your beautiful medical advice "go sit on the toilet" for any ailment from a stomachache to a headache.
I love you because my favorite meal is still fried chicken, rice, and creamed corn.
I love you for making the effort of ensuring my biological father remained in my life.

- I love you because I love him. He has made me into the man I am today.
- I love you for marrying and bringing amazing sisters into my life.
- I love you for all that you have done and continue to do for my life.

My song for mama is a message of thanks and love.
Mama, now you truly know, how much I love you.

Prose from a Soul Seeking Justice

Made in the USA
Columbia, SC
16 December 2023